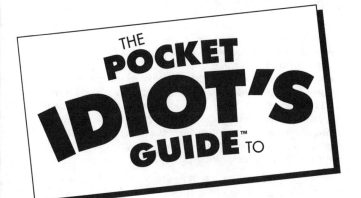

Being a Groom

by Jennifer Lata and Mark Rung

alpha books

Macmillan USA, Inc.
201 West 103rd Street
Indianapolis, IN 46290

A Pearson Education Company

Copyright © 1999 by Jennifer Lata

Alpha Development Team

Publisher
Marie Butler-Knight

Editorial Director
Gary M. Krebs

Associate Managing Editor
Cari Shaw Fischer

Acquisitions Editors
Randy Ladenheim-Gil
Amy Gordon

Development Editors
Phil Kitchel
Amy Zavatto

Assistant Editor
Georgette Blau

Production Team

Development Editor
Joan D. Paterson

Production Editors
Tammy Ahrens
Mike Thomas

Copy Editor
Kris Simmons

Cover Designer
Mike Freeland

Photo Editor
Richard H. Fox

Book Designers
Scott Cook and Amy Adams of DesignLab

Illustrator
Jody P. Schaeffer

Indexer
Chris Wilcox

Layout/Proofreading
Angela Calvert
Cheryl Lynch

Contents

Introduction

So You're Ready to Take the Plunge

We know you're no idiot. In fact, if you're reading this book, you must be pretty smart. That's because you're wise enough to know exactly what you *don't* know about—and that's weddings. It's okay that you don't know; you're not supposed to. Unlike your fiancée, you were not born and bred with the divine knowledge of all things nuptial—nor do you want to pore through book after thick bridal book looking for the information you need. Whether you're searching for ideas on gifts for your groomsmen, how to budget for a wedding (and beyond), or what you need to do to get a marriage license, we've compiled all the necessary information to be your one-stop resource.

Thirty years ago, you wouldn't have needed this book. Chances are your father had little or nothing to do with planning a wedding and frankly can't believe that you would, either. But as you know, times have changed—and whether your fiancée is a strict traditionalist or assumes the planning will be strictly 50/50, there's information in this book to help you. What better way to impress your bride than to tell her where the wedding ring originated? Or help her choose a photographer? Or even better, use one of our wedding gift suggestions for your bride?

How to Use This Book

The book is designed to offer all the information you need with the minimum effort necessary to get it. If you need advice on a certain topic, simply refer to the table of contents. If you need a serious but quick briefing on the bigger picture, take a breeze through each chapter. Within, you'll find the following features offering little snacks of information for the times you're not hungry for the whole enchilada.

Wedding Words

You haven't had this much trouble understanding another human being since 8th grade Spanish. Fear no more: Wedding Words are here to help you get to the bottom of confusing wedding jargon.

Groom Gambits

This is quick, bite-sized information that will provide you with money-saving, efficiency-gaining, and fool-proofing tips to sufficiently impress your bride, your family, and your future in-laws.

Nuptial No-Nos

You're engaged now, so you're probably accustomed to hearing the word "no"—or at least being told what to do. Well, this feature will tell you what *not* to do to avoid losing your shirt, losing respect—or losing your mind.

Acknowledgments

I would like to thank Mark, my own groom, who by fine example provided wonderful fodder and first-hand insight into the matters at hand. There's no one I'd rather have on my team. Thanks also to Jessica Faust, who remembered my love of bridal books and gave me the chance to be on the other side.

Trademarks

All terms mentioned in this book that are known to be or are suspected of being trademarks or service marks have been appropriately capitalized. Alpha Books and Macmillan USA cannot attest to the accuracy of this information. Use of a term in this book should not be regarded as affecting the validity of any trademark or service mark.

Chapter 1

So She's the One: Welcome to Couplehood

In This Chapter

➤ Why do I need a book?

➤ The definition of "groom"

➤ Exactly what components go into planning a wedding?

➤ Have I made the right decision?

Well, the hard work is over. You studied and scrutinized to find just the right engagement ring; you sweated and stuttered when talking to her father about your intentions; you even got down on bended knee and (although there's no need to admit this) shed a tear when she said yes. The rest is smooth sailing. All you have left to say is "I do" and head out for that honeymoon, right? Wrong!

You've got a long road ahead of you, and you've barely left the exit ramp. Being a groom means a lot more than just showing up these days. But hold on: I'm here to make this whole event as smooth as possible. So grab a beer, sit back, and prepare for the ride.

Why a Groom's Guide?

In just a generation or two, weddings and the preparation leading up to them have changed drastically. It's rare these days to experience what was normal in our parents' day—the blushing bride, barely (or not even) in her 20s, swept away by her handsome groom from her parents' home.

How Many Cattle Is Your Bride Bringing to the Marriage?

In the days when gender roles were more finely drawn, traditions developed: The bride's parents paid the lion's share of the wedding expenses, theoretically as a sort of *dowry* before her husband began supporting her financially.

Wedding Words

A **dowry** is historically an offering of cash, gifts, or a combination of both from the bride's family to the groom, to make the transaction more "worthwhile."

Of course, with the money also came most of the input and veto power. Traditions such as pre-wedding showers were in place to help the young couple set up their home with dishes, linens, and appliances. Nowadays, many couples already have two households full of most of the things they need. A pre-wedding pow-wow of the couple's parents used to be a way to introduce them to one another, as well as provide a forum to make any additional wedding-related financial arrangements. Today, this is more complicated, with more couples living far away from the places where they grew up, and with divorces and step-families complicating the issue even further.

Closing (or Retaining) Gender Gaps

With all the social changes of the past 30 or 40 years have come inevitable changes in wedding tradition—and particularly in the groom's wedding role. Formerly, most grooms left the planning to the brides and their families and showed up to events as they were told. But now, many grooms have more of a financial stake in their own weddings—and working women and their working mothers don't have the free time they once did to pore over guest lists and invitations for days on end. The tricky part comes with knowing when to adhere to tradition—and when to break it. This book is meant to help grooms work with their brides for an arrangement that will best suit their particular situations.

Groom Gambit

You should view your wedding planning much the same way you would view a project at work. When you begin partnering on a project with someone, you are generally a bit sensitive right away to the other person's working habits and style.

Use a strategy that works for you. In all likelihood, this is the largest "project" the two of you have worked on to date. With a little diplomacy and sensitivity, you'll figure out a system that works best for you as a couple. Your bride might want to plan every last detail and just let you show up; if that's okay with you, then go for it. However, your bride might really need your help.

What Is a Groom?

A groom is just a guy on his wedding day, right? Wrong. Traditional definitions of the word *groom* define him as an engaged man up to and including his wedding day and for some time afterward. This means that a groom's duties don't begin and end on his wedding day; rather, his commitment and responsibilities kick in from the moment he's engaged.

Wedding Words

The Webster's II New Riverside Pocket Dictionary has some other definitions for **groom**—"to make neat and trim, brush," and "to train." Funny how a word once reserved for the betterment of horses has transcended to include men getting married.

We know that until now you've probably experienced an extended adolescence that has entailed drinking with the boys until all hours, sleeping until noon when you feel like it, and "postponing" laundry and dishwashing until it's convenient or until mold grows on the dishes, whichever comes first—in general, the minimum effort necessary to maintain your three basic needs of food, shelter, and beer.

The Transition from Foal to Stallion

Here is where the "to train" part enters this whole groom thing. Certainly, you will not become Mr. Cleaver overnight; some residual bachelor revelry will almost certainly remain in your system. However, it is customary to add some semblance of responsibility to your life—a full-time job and all-night partying cut back to just one night a week—you know, the basics. If you want to be the "perfect" groom, now's the time to really shine for your bride and your in-laws-to-be. Work a little harder for that promotion so her dad will rest easy knowing she'll never want for that yearly trip South. Put her before your buddies every once in a while so she continues to believe she made the right decision. Stash a little money each month to save for the house or the couch you desperately need to replace. In other words, become the man you've always had buried somewhere deep within you.

Nuptial No-Nos

Don't assume that just because she's got the ring, your job is finished. Your bride will welcome—and appreciate—any assistance you can give her during wedding planning, even if it's just happily agreeing to looking at some reception sites with her. In other words, the courtship ain't over yet.

Of course, this preparation is the mental game involved in being a groom. There are all sorts of practical, day-to-day tasks you must complete, help out with, or at least consult upon. That activity is what this book will help you get straight.

Your Engagement—What's in Store

Women generally know a lot about what's involved in weddings well before they're engaged. They're socialized to know—and be excited about—all things nuptial.

Chances are your bride has already been closely involved in a friend's or sister's wedding, so she has a basic knowledge of what's necessary. But you—well, we know that you've probably done all you can to avoid the trappings of weddings until now. Not only is that girl stuff, but it is also very, very frightening. But now that you're planning your own wedding, we're sure you'll want all the requisite information to have the best party—and find the greatest deals—possible.

Check out this quick list of the elements of planning a wedding:

- ➤ Setting a date
- ➤ Setting a budget
- ➤ Introducing your parents to each other
- ➤ Choosing your best man
- ➤ Deciding on a number for your wedding party and choosing your groomsmen
- ➤ Attending an engagement party
- ➤ Creating a guest list
- ➤ Creating a wedding-day seating plan
- ➤ Registering for gifts
- ➤ Choosing a ceremony site
- ➤ Choosing a reception site
- ➤ Choosing the music
- ➤ Choosing the decorations and flowers
- ➤ Choosing your tux style
- ➤ Finding adequate wedding-day transportation (limousine or whatever)
- ➤ Finding and hiring a photographer
- ➤ Finding and hiring a videographer

➤ Choosing your reception menu items

➤ Choosing and purchasing a wedding band for your bride

➤ Choosing a wedding gift for your bride

➤ Planning the rehearsal dinner

➤ Acquiring a marriage license

➤ Getting a blood test

➤ Choosing a honeymoon destination and planning your honeymoon

➤ Finding a place to live

➤ Furnishing the place where you'll live

So you wondered why you need a book on this stuff? Don't fret; we break this stuff down for you, step-by-step, so that by the time your wedding rolls around you'll be the expert.

Did I Make the Right Decision?

Yeah, yeah, it just feels right, right? Plus she's been badgering you relentlessly for a ring for what seems at least as long as sitting through *The English Patient*. Take our quiz to see whether you're making the right decision:

1. The two of you have plans to go out Friday night with a group of friends; you get the flu. Does she

   A. Go out anyway and come in at 3 a.m., waking you up to tell you how much fun she had?

   B. Get mad at you for ruining your plans, and tell you you'd better start taking care of yourself?

   C. Come over to your place, make chicken soup, and put wet compresses on your head?

2. You forget to mention until Sunday morning that your mother has invited the two of you over for Sunday dinner. You know she doesn't have plans. Does she

    A. Refuse to go on principle?

    B. Go with you but pout and complain all night to the wonderment of your parents?

    C. Graciously accept the invitation?

3. It's Friday and the two of you have plans for dinner. Your best friend calls to tell you his fiancée has moved out of their apartment; she's met someone else. He really needs a shoulder right now. Does she

    A. Tell your friend you'll give him a call—after you get home from dinner and a movie?

    B. Reschedule your plans until Saturday so you two can talk?

    C. Make him dinner and set up your guest room for him for a few days so he won't be lonely?

4. Does she

    A. Call her father "Daddy" and refer often to his money?

    B. Call her father a "jerk" and obsess over him in tri-weekly sessions with her therapist?

    C. Call her father "Dad" and occasionally ask his advice or tell him she loves him?

5. Does a "night out with the girls" mean

    A. She shops for a week to find just the right provocative black cocktail dress?

    B. You'll have to hear the next day how she ran into Christopher, her old "friend" from college—"and he was wearing an Armani suit, and he just sold his business to Microsoft, and he *loves* opera?"

    C. Popcorn and *Ally McBeal* at her best friend's?

The scoring is very simple. If you answered one or more As or Bs, you might be in trouble, pal—or your fiancée's selfish behavior is the result of a communication breakdown between the two of you. All hope is not lost; read Chapter 5, "Fluctuating Emotions: And You Thought Once a Month Was Bad," for communication strategies useful for engagement and well beyond.

Walk in Her Shoes

According to most brides, the perfect groom is not a man who already knows everything he has to do: He's someone who understands the amount of work that goes into planning a wedding and who will be patient and communicative throughout the process. The perfect groom is also there to whisk her off for margaritas and dancing when things get too crazy after a long week extra hours at the office, an argument with a friend, and the DJ's announcement that he double-booked and can't provide the music for the wedding.

Keep in mind that patience is the key word during planning a wedding. She's going to be talking a lot about such things as colors, flowers, and her mother's dress—things as foreign to you as the Lifetime channel. Just hear her out and make suggestions about the stuff you do care about—the music, the limo, and budgetary decisions. She'll appreciate the input and the listening ear.

Groom Gambit

As an engaged man, you will slowly but surely witness the evolution of the pronoun "I" into "we" as you move closer to your wedding date. Seemingly this natural phenomenon has its roots in Darwinian theory—only the fittest survive.

Chapter 2

Pre-Game Strategy: Budgets You Can Work With

The games are about to begin. But first, you must develop a strategic plan (think Xs and Os on a blackboard, if that's easier) to be sure you're in the best possible shape for game day. Your bride and her family are the Xs; you and yours are the Os. It's tough to say exactly where the Xs are gonna end up at the end of each play, but you can create some possible scenarios to develop your counterattack. That's what you'll find in this chapter—"O" scenarios that are most comfortable for you, your bride, and your families.

But isn't this wedding stuff all about being on the same team? Eventually, yes. First, you've got to create the best possible situations for both parties—and then you're free to merge. Shift your thinking for a moment to consider two corporate entities merging. Before two companies come together, they're going make sure that both their interests are represented—especially those of a financial nature. Only then will the X company and O company become XO Inc.

Okay, enough with the sports/business/love metaphors and on to some concrete info.

Budgeting!

It's probably the first time you've seen budgeting and an exclamation point on the same page, right? We thought it might be nice to imbue some enthusiasm into a task that's about as palatable as a rice cake for dinner. Actually, budgeting doesn't have to be all bad (especially if the bride's parents have offered to foot the entire bill), but only if you treat it as you would any other financial arrangement—with practicality and good planning.

Groom Gambit

Before you and your bride even start putting figures in your budget, you need to decide just what type of wedding you're going to have and how much (if any) each set of parents is going to contribute.

After the heady glow of the first few days of engagement, your parents will probably bring up the subject of wedding finances. Traditional etiquette deems that the bride's parents pay for most of the wedding expenses, and the groom's pay for some additional items. Here's the traditional breakdown:

Bride and family:

➤ Engagement party (if one is held by bride's family)

➤ Groom's ring

➤ Wedding gift for the groom

➤ Paper items, including invitations, stationery, thank-you cards, and wedding programs (the printed booklets you have the option of giving guests at the ceremony)

➤ Bridal gown and mother's and father's wedding-day attire

➤ Flowers for church or temple and reception

➤ Bouquets for bridesmaids and flower girls

➤ Church or synagogue fees, ceremony music, and other ceremony expenses

➤ Wedding and engagement photography and videography

➤ Transportation of bridal party to ceremony and reception

➤ All reception costs, including food, drink, room or hall rental fees, decorations, and music

Groom and family:

➤ Engagement party (if one is held by groom's family)

➤ Bride's engagement and wedding rings

➤ Wedding gift for the bride

➤ Rehearsal dinner

➤ Groom's tuxedo and parents' attire

- ➤ Bride's bouquet, boutonnieres for groomsmen, and corsages for mothers and grandmothers
- ➤ Marriage license
- ➤ Clergy's fee
- ➤ Honeymoon

Additional expenses to share or divide:

- ➤ Both families can pay for the rehearsal dinner if the groom's family is unable bear the entire cost.
- ➤ The families might offer to purchase the bridesmaids' dresses and accessories and groomsmen's rentals.
- ➤ The bride's family may buy all the flowers.
- ➤ Both families may split photography and videography.
- ➤ Additional costs include transportation and lodging for out-of-town guests.
- ➤ The groom's family can offer to cover specific reception costs such as liquor and hors d'oeuvres.

Unless you're flying on the Concorde, staying at the Ritz-Carlton, and taking an extended trip for your honeymoon, it's pretty obvious that the expenses weigh heavily on the bride's family's side if you're following traditional etiquette.

What Does This Traditional Budget Stuff Mean to Me?

Here's where wedding planning on the brink of the millennium gets tricky. Like the breakdown in traditional planning duties, the breakdown in who pays for what isn't as clear-cut as it once was. A professional couple in their 30s might have the resources available to pay for their own wedding and might want to do so in order to retain all the decision-making control in planning their big day. More and more, as marrying couples get older and more resourceful, they're sharing some, if not all, of the costs of their weddings.

Groom Gambit

This is the first serious conversation about your wedding that you'll have with your bride—to determine what each family's contribution will be, if any, and to decide how you'll want to pay for it.

How to Approach Family

Presumably, your families are savvy enough to bring up the subject of *wedding finances* before you need to bring it up with them. Perhaps there's already a "financial understanding" in each of your families, based on older siblings who've had weddings. Maybe your bride's family has always communicated to her that they'll pay for her whole wedding. These are the easiest-case scenarios. But it can become uncomfortable if your parents never broach the topic, and you're left to wonder what, if any, they'll be willing to cover. This leaves you with a couple of options: You can either approach them (with delicacy and diplomacy) to see if they can swing anything or plan on paying for everything yourselves. Then, if they offer later, you'll be ahead of the game.

Wedding Words

When it comes to **wedding finances,** don't assume either
set of parents will pay for anything wedding-related until
they tell you so. Be sensitive to their financial situation,
and speak to them as an adult, not as a spoiled child
"entitled" to their patronage.

Nitty-Gritty Budgeting

Okay, here's the tough part. Wedding expenses range
drastically, depending on the type of wedding you're having, where you're having it, and how many people you're
inviting. You might be planning a simple backyard wedding with a punch-and-cookies reception or a traditional,
full-blown evening reception for 350 guests at the nicest
place in town. It's actually a catch-22: Budget dictates
what type of wedding you'll have, and what type of wedding you want will determine budget parameters. It's up
to you to decide whether the chicken or the egg comes
first.

Your first option is to decide what type of wedding you
want, factor in parental contributions, and determine how
much you'll need to save. Based on these calculations
you'll set a date to accommodate your savings plan.

Your other option, if you're paying for part or all of your
wedding, is to decide on a budgetary figure before you
even think about what type of wedding you want. For example, if together you want to spend $5,000, you can use
that figure to decide where you'll have it, what kind of
food and drink you'll have, and how many people you'll
invite. If you decide on 40 guests, $5,000 will buy you a

pretty elegant affair. If you want 250 guests, think more about the cookout range (or cocktails only).

Nuptial No-Nos

Don't forget that you and your bride have the ultimate power to decide what's important. Don't buy into every wedding service you see.

Here are some of the specific components you need to consider when budgeting for a traditional wedding. Obviously, each wedding is individual, and you can decide to eschew any of these items (or elope, for that matter). Beware of the fire hose level of pressure you'll encounter from the wedding industry, hawking their wares at an emotional time.

Costs vary widely for the following. Check with friends and local vendors for ballpark figures in your area, and then set your own parameters:

➤ Rehearsal dinner
➤ Ceremony fees, including clergy and musician's fees
➤ Reception food
➤ Reception bar
➤ Reception music (live versus DJ makes a huge financial difference)
➤ Wedding attire—bridal gown and formal men's attire
➤ Flowers and other decorative items (more expensive than you'd think)
➤ Photography and videography

➤ Transportation (limo from ceremony to reception, "getaway" car)

➤ Wedding invitations and thank-you stationery

➤ Wedding-day program

➤ Wedding bands

➤ Gifts for wedding attendants

➤ Gifts for each other

➤ Overnight accommodations for you and your bride

➤ Subsidizing bridal party expenses (unless you're a Rockefeller, it's not mandatory)

➤ Additional expenses (wedding favors, grooming expenses such as haircuts, and so on)

➤ Honeymoon

Choosing Your Wedding Style

There are as many types of weddings as potential brides to choose from (seemingly endless, but when it comes right down to it, quite limited by your sound practical judgment and parents' approval). Now that you've established your budget, you'll consider your options; in other words, you're not obligated to spend thousands of dollars on a generic hall punctuated by 200 guests, mediocre food, and your drunk college friends hitting on your (not-so-little-anymore) sister. Nor are you expected to max out your credit card and hock your stereo to pay for flowers that have a one-day life span. If you're lucky enough to have carte blanche, however, there are options here to suit you as well.

Some of your options include the following styles:

➤ **Outdoor.** An outdoor, casual wedding such as a clambake or cookout on the beach or at a park, with plenty of spirits, good friends, and family.

➤ **Small but elegant.** A small, elegant affair of less than 50 guests with immediate family and very close friends. Use the money you're saving from limiting guests on excellent food and an unforgettable venue.

➤ **Non-traditional.** A non-traditional site such as an art gallery, historical museum, or landmark that offers guests a unique experience they'll always remember.

➤ **Getaway.** A getaway wedding (becoming more popular), where you and close family and friends spend a week or long weekend somewhere tropical—with the getaway highlighted by your exchanged vows. You may offer to pay for some or part of your guests' costs in lieu of incurring traditional wedding expenses.

➤ **Weekend wedding.** Ideal for larger budgets and a lot of out-of-town guests. Give your guests a weekend they won't forget by hosting weekend-long events in addition to the traditional rehearsal dinner and wedding. Plan activities for the daytime such as a sight-seeing excursion, golf outing, beach party, or outdoor barbecue for your guests so they'll have something to do before and after the wedding festivities.

➤ **Cocktail/champagne.** A daytime cake-and-champagne-toast-only wedding or an evening cocktails-only reception to save money on food. (Be careful with this one; many guests expect to be served a meal at a wedding, so make it very clear on the invitation that there will be no brunch, lunch, or dinner. Also, be prepared for some whining.)

➤ **At home.** A home-catered event, with relatives and friends doing the cooking to save money.

Clearly, any variation of these styles can be combined with your own creativity to plan an event that fits both your budget and your personal style—an event that none of your guests will ever forget. Plus you'll avoid all that cookie-cutter, chicken-dance, I-can't-even-sit-with-my-date rigamarole.

Setting the Date

Now that you've got your projected budget and an idea of the type of wedding you want, it will be easier to set a date for the wedding. The following are some variables to consider when setting this all-important date that you'll celebrate for the next 50+ years (until you rejoin your gender and begin forgetting after a couple of anniversaries):

➤ **Season.** Time of year you prefer—winter, spring, fall, or summer. Keep in mind that if you don't have a long engagement, it's tougher to get the place, photographer, and band you want in late spring, summer, and early fall because that's when everyone else is getting married, too.

➤ **Location.** Where your wedding will take place. If it's out of town, be sure to establish enough time for long-distance planning and inevitable travel back and forth beforehand.

➤ **Timing.** How long you'd like your engagement to be (which is most vital in "shotgun" situations). In other, less intense situations, you should determine whether it's important to you to plan and marry right away or a job or personal considerations make it more practical to have a longer engagement.

➤ **Conflicts.** Other family events, such as relatives' weddings or milestone occasions like anniversaries, that could potentially conflict with your event. Be considerate: If your grandparents are inviting a lot of out-of-town guests for their 50th wedding

anniversary in August, don't expect those same
people to fly back to town in September.

➤ **Holidays.** Don't forget to consider a range of religious holidays if you are inviting guests of different
faiths. Consider that you might get more regrets if
you choose to hold your wedding on a holiday or
holiday weekend, when people may have other
plans.

Nuptial No-Nos

One groom insisted he and his bride plan their wedding
for December 31, 1999. That's great for close family and
friends—but more casual acquaintances would rather be
with *their* close family and friends on this historic occasion.
You'll get a lot of guests' regrets if you don't consider
others' priorities when setting a date.

Adding a Personal Touch

There are as many ways to make your wedding unique
as there are people who get married. If you think you're
stuck with a cookie-cutter wedding like the six you attended last year alone, think again. You are free to do
whatever you like to make your wedding more interesting
and memorable for you and for your guests. Little touches
can go a long way, especially if they reflect the personalities of you and your bride.

Take the following case histories into account when planning your own unique touches:

➤ One North Carolina couple had their ceremony on
the golf course—no, not in the clubhouse, on the

actual golf course. Both avid golfers, the bride and groom had met on the golf course when he was a pro giving her lessons. His connection at the course obviously helped out a bit in securing this valuable space, especially during prime season. But we know you, too, have a resourceful side.

➤ One couple who loved all things kitsch hired a karaoke guy to provide entertainment at their wedding. Once guests got warmed up, you couldn't keep them away from the microphone. Many stars were born that night—and crashed and burned the next day.

➤ One groom, an amateur musician, brought out his guitar during the ceremony and surprised his bride with a song he wrote for her, with all the guests in attendance as witnesses. The wedding was held in a state park with an outdoor, casual reception that mirrored the couple's unconventional lifestyle.

➤ One couple had a traditional ethnic Polish wedding, with events following dinner that included the groom wearing a traditional Polish hat and being raised and carried in his chair by his groomsmen. The Keystone Cops also paid a visit, and Polish food and music abounded.

Chapter 3

The Cast

In This Chapter

➤ Choosing your best man

➤ Traditional groomsman duties

➤ Other honorary positions

➤ Choosing clergy

➤ Creating a guest list

Whether you're usually a total attention-monger or a behind-the-scenes kinda guy, your wedding day will inevitably mean one thing: It's your bride's starring role, and you're the Spencer Tracy to her Katherine Hepburn. Be prepared for a lot of attention—as well as a dual role as casting director for some supporting roles such as best man, groomsmen, and all those lucky extras who'll be eating your food and drinking your wine.

Does My Best Man Have to Be Better?

The whole concept of choosing one best man goes against the general grain of guyness. Unlike girls, who grew up with the need to publicly identify their best friends du jour, guys are more content to hang with a group, avoiding titles and labels—although there generally is one person who he's closer to than the others. This can be a brother, a childhood friend, a cousin—even your father. This is your *best man*.

Wedding Words

The **best man** is the person closest to the groom, chosen to carry out helpful wedding-related duties and to provide support.

Choosing Your Best Man

The role of best man is charged with responsibility and reliability. The best man is much more high profile than the maid or matron of honor, if only because of the very public wedding-day speech he delivers. But the best man's duties don't start and end there. From a traditional standpoint, the best man's duties begin the day he accepts this responsibility. This is one of the few times in life when a guy is going to need a real "best friend," in the true sense of the word, to alleviate the stress of planning, dealing with his bride and in-laws, and preparing for the holy sanctity of lifelong marriage. Choose wisely. Don't choose your college drinking buddy who's always resented your fiancée for "taking you away from him." This combination has ugly engraved all over it. Don't choose your black-sheep brother just because you're related; the temptation might be too great for him to use your wedding as a public forum for his life-long grievances. One best man I know got so drunk that during his speech, he actually began insulting the bride, his parents, and his brother (the groom). His father had to physically pull him off "stage," and it seemed like an eternity until the tension lifted. You and your parents spend a lot of time, money, and energy to plan this wedding; you don't want to ruin it with some ill-chosen clod as your best man.

Choosing this fellow can also be a touchy process, especially if you're equally close to two friends, two brothers, or a brother and a friend. If it comes down to the third scenario, it's wise to default to the blood-is-thicker-than-water theory and choose your brother. Your friend should understand. But in the first two scenarios, you'll have to use some Kissinger-like diplomacy. Hey, you're getting married. You're a grown-up now; we know you can handle it.

Nuptial No-Nos

To avoid embarrassment, be sure to choose a best man who you can rely upon to act maturely and mirror your best interests. In other words, don't choose a best man who is known for his violent outbursts, who detests your bride, who is in love with your bride, or who thinks marriage is a pointless, archaic institution.

What Does Your Best Man Do?

Here are the best man's traditional duties:

➤ Act as moral support through the engagement process.

➤ Plan and execute the bachelor party.

➤ Deliver the groom in a timely fashion to the wedding ceremony.

➤ Carry and protect the wedding bands.

➤ Stand next to the groom during the ceremony.

➤ Act as an official witness to the exchange, signing the wedding certificate.

➤ (Optional) Give the clergy a "donation" on behalf of the groom.

➤ Prepare and provide a well-formed speech prior to (or immediately following) the wedding repast (and optionally, the rehearsal dinner).

The Best Man's Speech

We've heard some great speeches and some truly awful, awkward, uncomfortable ones. The person you choose as best man may not be a natural orator, but at least instill in him (or have one of the groomsmen instill in him) the importance of a little preparation beforehand. Whether he writes out some notes, practices in front of a mirror, or memorizes an entire speech, a good speech from the best man adds class and requisite sentimentality to your wedding.

Groom Gambit

Remind your best man that the wedding reception includes more than his Gen X buddies. He should tailor his speech to also appeal to the children, grandmas, and pregnant women in the room. Meaning no limericks or off-color jokes—or unseemly references to the bachelor party.

Here are some tips to share with your best man:

➤ **Keep it simple.** For the less experienced speaker, short and sweet make a speech easier to deliver and easier for the audience to follow and enjoy. Long, drawn-out anecdotes and complicated jokes should be avoided.

➤ **Do your homework.** Include anecdotes that are funny, flattering, or from the heart. Kept in good taste, a personal speech makes an audience more interested and receptive.

➤ **Write it down.** No one will fault you for subtly referring to index cards.

➤ **Practice.** Give the speech to a friend or your dog.

➤ **Don't drown your fears.** One drink might calm your nerves, but five will make you incoherent. Lay off the booze until *after* the speech.

The Bachelor Party

Depending on your bride, the bachelor party will invoke different levels of distaste and distrust. But no rational woman loves thinking about your reverting to Cro-Magnon man, getting as drunk as humanly possible while watching women in various stages of undress. Of course, you'll plead innocence because theoretically your best man is in charge; he's the one planning it, and you have to go along with whatever he's planned, right? Hint: You're marrying your bride presumably because she's smarter than that. She's still going to hold you responsible for any misdeeds.

If you don't want the heat, make sure it's clear to your best man that he stay out of the kitchen. Or at the very least, make sure that what happens in the kitchen stays in the kitchen. You don't want a major blow-up the week before the wedding, as with one couple we know whose best man was called the morning after the bachelor party and told by the bride he would no longer be a welcome part of the wedding. Reportedly, he arranged for some "activities" at the bachelor party that she found…well, distasteful. They managed to mend fences in the week leading up the wedding, but some residual hard feelings and injured egos remained. So, tread carefully. We discuss more about bachelor parties in Chapter 6, "Pre-Wedding Events."

Do Groomsmen Have to be Well-Groomed?

The same caveats for choosing a best man apply to choosing groomsmen. Pick close relatives and good friends only—guys you think you have a good chance of knowing in 10 years. It's nice to include her brothers, but it's only necessary if you're close to them. You might have to include someone out of obligation; unless he's a potential troublemaker, suck it up. One groom even had his best girlfriend in the groomsmen's party. The theory is to make this as smooth an operation as possible, without creating life-long enemies or injured egos.

Groom Gambit

Choose among your more responsible, mature friends and family as groomsmen. You don't want to have to badger them to get fitted for formalwear or worry they're sleeping off a bender on the morning of your wedding.

Here are the groomsmen's traditional duties:

➤ Provide moral support during the engagement.

➤ Attend the rehearsal and rehearsal dinner.

➤ Arrive on time at the church or temple.

➤ Usher guests to their seats.

➤ Sit at the reception bridal table.

➤ Endure the long photography session (with you!).

Groomsmen are also free to give a toast at the rehearsal dinner.

Other Honorary Positions

Suppose your bride enlists only four bridesmaids. She's insisting that your *attendants* equal hers in number, so the pictures are "balanced." But you can't ask Richie without asking Potsie, Ralph, and Chachi—and your two brothers are *groomsmen,* too. What's a guy to do?

Wedding Words

What's the difference between **attendants, groomsmen, ushers,** and the **best man**? The best man *is* a special groomsman. The groomsmen act as ushers, seating people at the wedding and rolling out the runner for the bride to walk down. They're all considered attendants. You'll hear these terms used interchangeably.

You can avoid snubbing the other special people in your life by assigning some honorary tasks, such as reading passages during the ceremony, bringing gifts to the altar, or serving as extra *ushers.* Keep in mind that your bride might want to assign some of these positions, too, even if she is being unreasonable about the number of attendants. You can also be creative and make up new honorary positions; a male version of the "personal attendant" can make sure that your socks match, your tie is on correctly, and your shaving nicks have stopped bleeding. A "bartender" can make sure the limo is stocked for the ride after the ceremony and can ride with you to the reception. (Think the Fonz). It's your day: You and your bride can do what you want to make as many people as you choose a special part of the festivities.

Ask your clergyman about other honorary positions at the ceremony.

Choosing Clergy

If you're having a civil ceremony only, you can ignore this section. But if you're having a religious ceremony, read ahead; you have a few options. First, you'll decide with your bride where the ceremony will take place—in a church, temple, outdoors, and so on (or she'll decide for you). This choice may be a given if you've both belonged to the same church or temple your whole lives.

You then have the option of being married by the clergy serving that venue or asking a clergy member who's a relative or close family friend to do the honors. Your parents will probably bring this up if it's a priority. You might not necessarily be able to substitute your clergy for the clergy in attendance at the site you choose. But you should weigh these options with your family. It's appropriate to invite this clergy member to both the rehearsal dinner and the reception, where he or she can also give a special blessing.

The Guest List

Ah, the guest list. It's the time you must decide, in writing, who makes the final friendship cut and who doesn't. It'll be there for all the world to see. Sound like fun?

The guest list is probably one of the most difficult things you personally will be charged with preparing for the wedding. There are never enough open spots, it seems, to fit in your family, childhood friends, high school friends, college friends, work pals, and golf buddies, without going into debt for life. Somehow, you'll have to finesse this list.

The best thing to do is to start with an unequivocal number, a number you, your bride, and your families agree upon in advance. Depending on who's footing most of the bill, this could be wholly up to you, or you might be at the mercy of your bride and her family, who will give you a number to work with (usually around half the total guest list). You'll then need to talk to your parents about who they want to invite among their family and friends and at the same time coordinate your own list of friends and business associates. Unless your family is footing half the bill, it's rude for you—or them—to insist on inviting more people than the agreed-upon number.

Groom Gambit

If you and your bride are paying for the reception costs, it's up to you how many people you want to invite. Work within your budget to figure out a final head count. Establish a number before you start creating your list, or things can quickly get out of hand.

Unless you have an unlimited budget, you'll probably have to make some tough choices. The nice thing about being the groom is that you can blame it on the bride if offended acquaintances question you: "Her family is throwing a small wedding." And you don't have to invite every person whose wedding you've attended, especially if your wedding is going to be on the smaller side. People understand that weddings are an expensive proposition. If they act ungraciously, they really weren't good friends in the first place.

Guest List Strategies

One strategy for inviting more people: If your parents are paying the reception costs, offer to pay for each extra person you want to invite above and beyond the guest count you've agreed upon. At a national average of about $50 a head for food and liquor, you might rethink inviting that freshman roommate you haven't talked to since graduating college or the guy across the hall you talk hockey with.

Another option: Create an "A" list and a "B" list. (Keep these lists close to the vest.) When you receive the inevitable A list declines, start sending invitations to the B list. Warning: This can get tricky. Time it so B-listers are asked as soon as possible after the original invitations go out, and make sure they have as little contact with A-listers as possible. A B-lister, even if he wants to come to your wedding, doesn't want to know he's a B-lister. (Warning: You might be accused of tackiness by more conservative types.)

Nuptial No-nos

When cutting names from your guest list, don't start with family. Traditional etiquette advises to cut business acquaintances first, then friends, and then family.

One more option is inviting people without inviting their dates. Presumably, you'll invite established couples of whom you know both halves, but the theory is that if a friend or family member doesn't have a current squeeze, you invite him or her singly. This can be problematic if your buddy claims he's met the girl of his dreams a month before your wedding—the seventh girl of his dreams since college, according to your calculations. It can be awkward deciding whose better half is "serious" enough to warrant inviting. But if you've got a few friends with absolutely no romantic entanglements, invite them alone. They might just get lucky with a single bridesmaid, anyway.

Of course, this option is not an excuse to disinvite Joe's girlfriend Marcia, who you've always found distasteful. It takes a bit of diplomacy to make this arrangement work. You can expect complaints even under the best of conditions—or at the very least, passive-aggressive response cards. A guy in Chicago was invited alone but sent his response card indicating "two" would be attending. This is just plain rude, of course, but you'll have to get used to major etiquette breaches; after all, not everyone has a book to guide their way.

Chapter 4

Let the Games Begin: Planning the Details

In This Chapter

➤ Choosing the ceremony and reception sites

➤ What to look for in a photographer

➤ Choosing your music

➤ Special transportation

➤ Girl stuff—flowers, stationery, and the bridal registry

So your pre-game plan is complete—you've got your budget, you've got your best man, you've got your ushers—and you've already got a headache. Depending on how things have gone so far, you're aware of just how much more you're going to get involved in the party planning. Your bride and her mother may have everything totally under control—and that's okay with you. Or you might find you like putting in your two cents—especially if you're contributing a lot more than that to the budget.

Whatever the case, this chapter is an overview of some of the specific elements that will need addressing well before wedding day, with a special emphasis on the stuff you care more about.

Get Me to the Church (or Chuppah) on Time

Choosing the site of your ceremony is easy if you and your bride met in church; you probably can come to a pretty easy conclusion about where your wedding is going to take place. But if you have two different faiths, live far away from your hometowns, or practice no religion, the question becomes more complicated. Traditionally, the bride and her family chose the wedding site because they were footing the bill. But if that's not the case, or you want to choose something a bit more unusual, you've got some options:

Traditional wedding sites:

➤ The college chapel of your alma mater

➤ The church or temple you've attended all your life

➤ The church or temple you've joined together

➤ The stunning church or temple your bride has always dreamed of marrying in

➤ Your reception site—a room adjacent to the hotel ballroom or the garden outside the reception hall

➤ A public park

➤ Your own home or a relative's

Creative wedding sites:

➤ A yacht

➤ A ballpark

➤ A museum or art gallery

➤ Under a beautiful tent on your rich uncle's estate

➤ A hot-air balloon

➤ Under water

➤ The beach

➤ The slopes

➤ The golf course

One unforgettable wedding we attended was in an intimate, open-air theater, with a reception following in a beautifully appointed barn with white-washed walls, formal table settings, and candlelight. The rustic yet semiformal atmosphere lent the wedding a completely unique atmosphere.

Interfaith Ceremonies

You're Catholic, she's Jewish. If you thought you could only have a civil ceremony, you're wrong. With any luck, one of the following options will calm even the most irate family member:

➤ Combine both faiths with co-officiating clergy. If your clergy is reluctant to participate, seek out college chaplains or more liberal-minded clergy in your area.

➤ Turn to a tolerant third religion, such as the Unitarian Church, which encourages couples to structure services that reflect both religions.

➤ Choose one religion over the other.

➤ Plan two weddings, one in each faith. (One could happen on a day separate from your larger reception day.)

Groom Gambit

Planning the ceremony can be the most sensitive issue of your wedding. Even laissez-faire parents can become incensed if you plan something non-traditional. Prepare in advance for opposition to proposed plans, especially if your parents or grandparents are devoutly religious and you're marrying outside the faith.

Party Time

So you've gotten through planning the ceremony, without offending too many people. Now, it's time to plan the fun part—the reception. Contrary to popular belief, there are many kinds of receptions, so it's up to you to choose what style, length, and formality you prefer. You might want to consolidate the ceremony and reception site at one location so guests won't have to travel or kill time in between. Or if that's not an option, have the ceremony and reception in separate locations. No matter what you choose, allow it to be a reflection of your—and your bride's—own personal style.

Depending on your budget and preferences, you have a number of choices. For a more subdued, shorter affair with limited expenses, you may choose to have a cake-and-punch reception, where there is no formal meal served. To limit costs for an evening occasion, have an hors d'oeuvres reception with a limited bar. If you choose either of these options, be sure guests know ahead of time; at the majority of today's weddings, guests expect a full meal. You don't want them starving and cranky when they find out there's only finger food at your reception.

Nuptial No-Nos

If you're having a reception with a limited meal or no meal, be sure guests know ahead of time. Most guests assume they will be fed at a wedding reception and may be upset if they come to your wedding hungry.

More elaborate, traditional receptions feature full meals. You can choose either buffet or sit-down-style meals, depending on your preferences. *Food-station receptions,* a variation of the traditional buffet, have also become popular. Instead of everyone eating at one time, food stations are out in separate areas of the room for a couple of hours and may include more contemporary fare such as stir-fry and fajitas in addition to traditional carving stations.

Wedding Words

With **food stations,** receptions are typically like cocktail parties—less structured with a bar that generally stays open all evening and no defined place settings. Just don't forget to eat!

Sit-down dinners can range from a very formal, five-course meal to a meal that's less formal with fewer courses. Your style will depend on local custom, budget, and personal preference.

Of course, you can also forgo the traditional dinner reception in favor of a beach barbecue, park picnic, or a day at the ballpark. Guests might find it a refreshing change, and you might find that it's more relaxed and reflective of your personalities.

Smile—You're Far from Candid Camera

For many grooms, the photography session can be a real drag. You're forced to stand stiffly, sweating in your formalwear for an exorbitant amount of time while your friends are just a spitting distance away, enjoying cocktails and regaling each other with old college stories. Hey, isn't this *your* wedding day? Come to think of it, do you really even want these pictures anyway?

Once your wedding day is history and all you have are fond but dim memories, you will appreciate your wedding photos. Actually, you'll probably even want some kind of say in choosing a photographer so you don't end up with some guy who's at best condescending and at worst downright irritating.

Nuptial No-Nos

It may be tempting to choose a friend or other amateur to take your wedding photos to save on cost, but don't leave such important photographs to chance. You've only got one shot to preserve these once-in-a-lifetime moments.

Here are some things to consider when choosing a photographer:

> ➤ Choose a professional with solid experience, top-of-the line equipment, and good lighting who will

efficiently guide your group to pose for all appropriate photos. Ask friends, your caterer, and parents for referrals, and view samples of the photographer's previous work before you book him.

➤ Take some posed shots so you're sure to include all close family members, the wedding party, and as many guests as possible.

➤ Encourage candid shots, or choose a photographer who specializes in photojournalistic style, catching spontaneous and emotional moments rather than only posed, formal shots.

➤ Place portable cameras on each table for guests to photograph each other.

➤ Be sure to get a signed contract with the details on cost and the amount of time the photographer will spend at the wedding.

When and if you also choose a videographer, use the same tips and beware of any additional editing or creative costs you might incur, based on the videographer's style.

The Wedding Singer

You saw the movie. A guy with a bad voice and hair that's short-in-front-long-in-back sings hot tunes from the '80s and woos Drew Barrymore. Now it's up to you and your bride to find similar entertainment for your shindig. Warning: Although this movie was a sentimental look back at another decade, as well as a comedy, there are still guys out there doing weddings who look and sing like Adam Sandler's character (without Adam's charm).

Our point? Choose your music carefully, whether it's live or not. Make sure you've had a chance to see your musician or DJ in action ahead of time. And think twice about taking your parents' band recommendations as gospel. Then again, they might just know something about music that transcends time and generations. Just be sure to check it out ahead of time.

The same goes for a DJ. We've been to a wedding or two where the DJ himself becomes the "entertainment" instead of the music he's supposed to be playing. Some DJs tend to make themselves the center of attention at a wedding, cracking bad jokes about the bride and groom and creating irritating games for guests to play. Don't let some frustrated performer make your wedding his personal stage—unless, of course, you like bad jokes and irritating games. Some other things to remember:

➤ When choosing a band or DJ, it's best to start with referrals from friends and family.

➤ Think carefully before employing your cousin's garage band just to save some cash. Chances are your guests won't like them quite as much as you do, and a wedding is a serious first gig for cousin Eddie to play.

➤ Sometimes, a band can vary its number of performers. If this is the case, consider having fewer band members to save some money. Be sure to listen to the scaled-down version before you book them, however.

➤ Check with the band to see whether they provide a sound system to keep playing music when they're taking breaks.

➤ When using a DJ, create a list of songs you'd like to hear and give it to him before the day of your wedding.

➤ If you'd like the DJ or bandleader to introduce your wedding party or perform other announcements, give this information to him or her ahead of time.

➤ Be sure to get everything in writing, including the cost, the amount of time they'll perform, and what type of retribution you'll get if they cancel. (It's been known to happen.)

Groom Gambit

Don't forget to give your band or DJ a list of songs to play during special dances such as the mother/son, father/daughter, and couple's first dance. First dance songs can come from any era, like "Can't Help Falling in Love" by Elvis Presley, "How Sweet It Is" by James Taylor, "It Had To Be You," by Frank Sinatra, or "True Companion" by Marc Cohn.

Ceremony and Cocktail Hour Music

Aside from your after-dinner dance music, you'll also need to choose music for your ceremony and cocktail hour.

For your ceremony, you'll want to speak with the music director at your church, temple, or ceremony site. He or she has done this many times before and will have a good idea of what you'll need. There are more options besides the traditional wedding march when your bride walks down the aisle, and music can be incorporated to be a large part of the ceremony.

For your cocktail hour, you've got some options. You might want to hire some separate musicians to play, such as a string quartet, piano player, or harpist. One wedding we attended featured a strolling violinist during dinner, who would play guests' requests. Another wedding simply had piped-in music from a sound system. Of course, it might be cost prohibitive to hire two groups of live music, so talk to your caterer or reception site manager to find out whether they have any other options, such as a built-in sound system.

Wheels

You've always wanted to ride in an antique Rolls? Or a stretch Lincoln Navigator with the works? Now's your chance (and possibly the only time your new wife will agree to such automotive extravagances). On your wedding day, you might not want to worry about driving yourself around. And you'll probably want to ride to your reception with the traveling party that are your groomsmen and bridesmaids. Between the stress of the wedding, a couple of drinks, and a long day, either designate someone the day's or evening's driver, or hire a chauffeur. If you prefer to use your own car, opt for the traditional "getaway" car, which the ushers may choose to "decorate" during the reception.

Groom Gambit

Check out the exteriors and interiors of the cars you'll be hiring to make sure they're in good shape and can seat the proper number of people.

If you do hire limousines or other cars, be sure to remember a few things:

➤ Book it six months ahead of time.

➤ Comparison shop for the best price.

➤ Be sure the company is a licensed, above-board operation. Check with the Better Business Bureau or only hire from referrals.

➤ Meet the driver, and choose your specific car ahead of time. Specify it in the contract.

➤ Be sure to provide the proper information to the company ahead of time, including pick-up locations, times, and whether the cars should wait between each destination.

➤ Find out about recourse if a car breaks down or it isn't the one you contracted.

Girl Stuff

Other components involved in planning a wedding include flowers, stationery, and church decorations. Unless you're a florist or an interior decorator, you probably won't want to be overly involved in these decisions. The following outlines strictly the basics.

Flowers

Flowers are expensive. If you're contributing financially to your wedding, don't underestimate the cost of flowers. Obviously, costs will vary, depending on whether you choose centerpieces of tropical flora on every table or simple bowls of wildflowers. Plan to spend more than you'd likely ever estimate.

Stationery

Stationery necessities include the invitation itself, the inserts regarding reception information, the reply card, and another stamped envelope. You will also need to budget for place cards, thank-you cards, and a *wedding program* (which is optional).

One groom, a writer from Buffalo, NY, fashioned his wedding program into a playbill entitled "Til Death Do Us Part," by "Jack & Mary Productions." Inside were profiles on the "cast members" and their "story"—the history of how they met. It made guests feel more personally involved in the wedding.

Wedding Words

A **wedding program** contains information about the ceremony readings and music, as well as such fun reading as wedding attendant profiles. The program can be customized as creatively as you'd like.

Stationery can also be expensive, especially if you're printing a lot of invitations or you are using more extravagant touches like engraving. A great way to save money is to get invitations through mail order; check out your fiancée's bridal magazines, which are crawling with ads from stationers.

Decorations

Leave the decorating to your bride and her mother. I promise you won't regret it—unless their taste is so god-awful or ostentatious that you find it absolutely necessary to interject. But you wouldn't be marrying a woman with bad taste, anyway, would you?

As one April '99 groom from New York City said: "Be warned. If you offer up an opinion on every little thing, your fiancée will then feel free to assume you want to be included in every maddening little detail of the wedding. Believe me, NASA put less effort into putting a man on the moon than your fiancée and future mother-in-law are putting into this wedding."

If you wash your hands of something, such as flowers, then stick with it. Don't jump in later with "I hate posies."

Traditional Duties of the Groom

We've mentioned a lot of wedding-related planning in this chapter. Now, there's a chance that the only thing you want to be involved in wedding-wise is what you absolutely have to be. In other words, you want to follow the dictates of traditional etiquette—in other words, less than what's implied in the rest of this book. If this is the case, we think the following section alone justifies the price of this book. Especially when you show it to your bride, and tell her that it means you're off the hook for a bunch of other stuff.

Timeline of duties traditionally assigned the groom:

Six months before the wedding:

➤ Decide the division of financial obligations.

➤ Set a budget.

➤ Set an appointment with the clergy.

➤ Prepare your guest list.

➤ Choose your best man and ushers.

➤ Plan your honeymoon.

➤ Check passports and visas.

Four months before the wedding:

➤ Buy wedding rings and order engraving.

➤ Select formalwear.

➤ Find a new place to live. (Yes, you will have to abandon roommates Brendan and Rodney forever.)

➤ Shop for new home furnishings (or start begging family members for giveaways).

➤ Make reservations for the honeymoon.

➤ Find lodging for out-of-town guests.

➤ Have a complete physical exam and update your immunizations.

➤ Set an appointment for the blood test.

Two months:

➤ Set a date with your fiancée to get the marriage license.

One month:

➤ Make reservations for the rehearsal dinner.

➤ Select your bride's gift and gifts for the attendants.

➤ Review legal, medical, and church documents.

➤ Confirm honeymoon details and reservations.

Two weeks:

➤ Move belongings to your new home.

➤ Have a bachelor party or dinner.

One week:

➤ Confirm the time and place of the wedding rehearsal and rehearsal dinner with all the attendants.

➤ Give the final guest count to the rehearsal dinner restaurant.

➤ Pick up wedding rings.

➤ Pick up your formalwear.

➤ Give the best man the clergy's fee in a sealed envelope for delivery.

➤ Pack for the honeymoon.

Whew, that still seems like a lot, doesn't it? But that doesn't even touch upon any of the actual party planning aspects, such as the reception, music, flowers, stationery…the list goes on. Consider how lucky you are to be male, and think of how proud and happy your bride will be if you actually do these things without being asked a minimum of three times first.

Chapter 5

Fluctuating Emotions: And You Thought Once a Month Was Bad

In This Chapter

- ➤ Holding on to your sanity
- ➤ Same-planet communication strategies
- ➤ She says/she means
- ➤ Inter-family communications
- ➤ Preparing for some major life changes

When you proposed, you made her a very happy woman—congratulations. Hold on to that elation because the most ironic part of weddings is that in preparing for the happiest day of her life, she might have some of the worst—or at least the most pressure-filled. Conflicting opinions, unexpected situations, demanding in-laws, time pressures—any number of situations can combine to heighten her stress and thus yours. Not to mention you've just made one of the most important decisions of your life, so you might be a little further from carefree than you're used to. But there's hope; plenty of lesser men have gone through it before you. This chapter is your personal troubleshooting guide to getting through the rough spots. Without shooting anybody.

I Am a Rock

As you've probably deduced by now, planning a wedding is no easy task. Even if your fiancée is an event planner by profession, she's going to experience stress from planning this party like she's had with none other. The reason? They are many and varied, but the gist of it is the cult of weddings: This is supposed to be the happiest day of her life, full of good weather, great food, and wonderful friends and family who all get along perfectly. Already it's easy to see where disappointment and frustration loom.

Chances are she's probably handling more of the details than you are in planning this event. If you got off lucky and you don't have to handle much outside the traditional groom stuff, here's your chance to shine. Be the man she's always dreamed of. Be her rock.

How to Be a Rock

It's hard to explain how to be a rock in a few simple words. It's more a way of life, a way of thinking best described by personal anecdotes. The following are some real-life wedding horror stories and how these grooms of stone helped handle them:

> ➤ One Connecticut bride came down with Lyme disease three months before her wedding. Although the majority of planning was complete, the remaining pre-wedding tasks included fitting the dress, picking up stationery, meeting with musicians, meeting with the caterer, choosing and picking up favors,

and so on. She was bedridden for two full weeks and still weak for a long time afterward—but her groom came to the rescue, running the errands she was unable to, helping address invitations, putting together favors, and meeting with the caterer. He even convinced the tailor to come to her house for her first fitting. Her friends and family were duly impressed.

➤ One bride in San Francisco nearly had a nervous breakdown when her band called a month before the wedding to cancel. At that short notice, she thought she'd never get a decent replacement for the wedding. The groom took matters into his own hands, calling on a friend who was currently touring with a band just on the verge of making it big. The band's days of performing weddings were long gone, but the groom managed to convince his friend and the band to make this one, last, wedding appearance. It cost him a little cash, but the rewards far outweighed the cost when he saw how pleased his bride was—and how excited the guests were to have their own private concert.

➤ When one Minnesota bride was laid off from her high-profile chef's position a few weeks before her wedding, she was understandably crushed to have to worry about getting a new job when all she wanted to think about was her upcoming wedding. Her groom convinced her to take this opportunity to start the catering business she had always dreamed about—and to put off worrying about it until *after* the wedding. He even offered to back her financially and support the two of them until she got her business off the ground.

The moral of the story? When things go wrong, it's your time to shine. As they say, take the ball and run with it.

Same-Planet Communication Strategies

If you've dated for a while, chances are you and your bride have had at least a few disagreements and have developed a basic pattern of working through them. You cannot underestimate the value of good communication in the pursuit of a strong marriage, especially when dealing with disagreements or conflicting interests. The engagement period is as good a time as any to brush up on these skills, especially because it's often rife with disagreements and conflicting interests. We describe the basic elements of "active listening" or "mirroring," a proven method of healthy, *constructive communication.*

Wedding Words

The techniques that contribute to **constructive communication** in this section come from the experts at the Relationship Institute. You can find more information about the Relationship Institute at www.relationship-institute.com or by calling 248-546-0407.

The four major blocks to healthy communication that couples adopt in their interactions are

1. Arguing or withdrawing
2. Blaming and accusing
3. Not listening
4. Changing the subject

By using these blocks to good communication, a couple virtually ensures that they will not be able to resolve conflicts. Suppose you have plans to take your fiancée to dinner, and at 4:00 your best friend calls to offer a free ticket to the basketball game. To you, it's a no-brainer: You've gotta go to the b-ball game, which was sold out weeks ago. But your fiancée isn't going to be happy, and you know that ahead of time. Such a situation requires finesse, and the following sections present some strategies to help you avoid major conflict.

Set the Stage for Healthy Communication

For good communication to occur, you must choose the right time and place. If either of you is too upset or distracted, one of the four communication blocks will most likely end up hindering the discussion.

If you or your bride is too upset to have a constructive conversation, do the following:

1. Stop and cool down; leave the situation if necessary for a while.
2. Set a specific time and place to talk again.
3. Don't interrupt her; let her finish her thoughts.
4. Acknowledge her concerns.

Use "I" Messages

Instead of blaming or accusing, starting sentences with "you always" or "you never," it's best to take responsibility for what you are feeling and communicate it to your fiancée. If you begin your sentences with "I feel" or "I think," she'll be less likely to immediately jump to the defensive.

To put this strategy into action

1. Discuss your feelings in a responsible way.
2. If you discuss your fiancée's behavior, do so in terms of your feelings.
3. Let your fiancée know your feelings when she engages in the behavior.
4. Tell her the consequences of her behavior to you.

For instance, if you're upset when she doesn't call when she's coming home late, your first instinct might be to blame and accuse, saying, "You're irresponsible," "You don't care about me," or "You're selfish." Using "I" statements, the same statement might come out like this: "When you stay out late, past the time you told me you'd be home, I feel hurt, frustrated, and angry. When you do come home, I really don't want to be close with you. In fact, it usually takes me a full day before I feel like spending time with you again."

Use Active Listening

With active listening, the listener's job is strictly to listen, without interruption and without adding anything to what the speaker has said.

The key elements of active listening are to

> ➤ **Listen to understand.** Even if you don't agree with what your fiancée is saying, pay attention and listen to it.

> ➤ **Summarize.** After you've heard her, paraphrase and repeat back what you heard. "So what I heard you say was…."

> ➤ **Verify.** When you are done summarizing what you heard, ask her, "Did I hear you correctly?" Let her give you feedback. Maybe you missed an important element of what she said. This isn't a test of right or wrong; it's about listening and making sure everyone is heard.

> ➤ **Be open and receptive for more input.** When she has agreed that you have heard her correctly on that one comment, ask her, "Is there anything else you want to say?" Let her know that she has the floor until she's finished getting everything off her chest.

Stay on One Subject at a Time

By agreeing ahead of time to talk about only one topic
and nothing else, couples can make significant progress
on an issue. It might take several sessions to hear what the
other has to say about a topic, just as it took some time
for the feelings about the topic to develop. Be patient and
keep talking. And give her this chapter to read, too.

I Am Woman, Hear Me Roar...or Just Hear Me

Some fundamental differences between men and women
can lead to conflict. By recognizing them, you can make a
first step toward resolution.

Following are some of those differences:

➤ The most frequent complaint men have about
women: Women are always trying to change them.

➤ The most frequent complaint women have about
men: Men don't listen.

➤ Women want empathy, whereas men are more
solution-oriented.

➤ When a woman tries to change, improve, correct, or
give a man advice, the man interprets it as being
told he is incompetent or can't handle something
alone.

➤ Men often feel responsible or blamed for women's
problems.

➤ Men assume that the best way to be helpful to
women is to offer advice or solutions to their problems; women often just want someone to sincerely
listen to them.

Groom Gambit

Be sure to keep in mind the fundamental differences between men and women when communicating about anything important, when expressing care and concern, and when solving conflicts.

➤ When women are upset, it's not the time to offer solutions; that is more appropriate at a future time when she's calmer.

➤ A man appreciates advice and criticism when it is requested. Men want to make improvements when they are approached as a solution to a problem rather than the problem itself.

➤ Men have great needs for status and independence (emphasis on separate and different); women have needs for intimacy and connection (close and same).

➤ Women need to experience caring, understanding, respect, devotion, validation, and reassurance.

➤ Women are motivated when they feel special or cherished.

➤ Men need to experience trust, acceptance, appreciation, admiration, approval, and encouragement.

➤ Men are motivated when they feel needed. A man's deepest fear is that he is not good enough or not competent enough, although he might never express this.

These differences are not better or worse, just different. Of course, these are generalizations; differences occur in all of us, and most of us carry some combination of "masculine" and "feminine" traits. To get along, however, you both must accept, expect, and respect these differences.

When you approach the unavoidable conflict regarding the basketball game, perhaps you should offer a promise of something extra special the next day, reassure her that you respect her and your plans, and acknowledge that you hate to miss dinner with her but you also hate to pass up this opportunity. With any luck, she'll respect your need for independence, and trust you'll make good on your next-day promise for something even better.

Inter-Family Communication

You can use the communication strategies presented here with anyone, not just your fiancée. When it comes to communicating with your in-laws-to-be, however, all bets are off. The clichés about in-laws exist for a reason.

Nuptial No-Nos

Though she may complain about her family until she's blue in the face, it's up to you to never, ever offer an unsolicited criticism of her relatives. This illogical rationale will become one of the fundamental tenets of your marriage.

An important point to remember now that you're getting married is that you're not only marrying your fiancée; you're also marrying her family. Her brother doesn't have to fill the role of your new best friend, but it'll save you a life's worth of headaches if you make some effort now to get along with her family. If you already have a great relationship, good for you. You can stop reading now. If you don't, here are some surefire strategies for dealing with different types of in-laws.

The Over-Involved

You figure they must be really bored because in addition to living their own lives, they're also trying to live yours. Either that or they're control freaks. This type of in-law is characterized by dropping in without warning, making plans for you without asking, assuming everything, and appeasing no one. Great diplomacy is necessary on your part, but you'll probably want to nip this over-indulgence in the bud before it spirals madly out of control and you wake up to discover you're building an in-law apartment off your living room. Sometimes, you just have to say no, even if you're trying like mad to please them and display what a great guy you are.

The Under-Involved

These in-laws barely know your name, and you get the feeling it might take a few years before her dad actually has a conversation with you. Consider yourself lucky. Unless he genuinely doesn't like you, he's probably just distracted by work, gardening, golf—who really cares, as long as he's not distracted by you. If you're searching for a father figure, look elsewhere, but if you're happy to slide into a situation unnoticed, it's your lucky day.

The You're-Not-Quite-Good-Enough

When she's daddy's girl, daddy can be hard to please. He might not verbalize it overtly, but his grunts and one-word answers signify to you his disapproval. If you believe it's totally unfounded—that he's basing his judgment on some superficialities beyond your control—take on the challenge of winning him over during the engagement period. That doesn't mean shameless brown-nosing; sometimes strong, silent actions are more effective. Show him how much you love his daughter in the little things you do, and make him confident that you will be a supportive husband and good provider. That's all daddy really cares about. (And whether you're already sleeping with his daughter.)

The Tug-of-War Family

Mom hates Dad. Dad hates Mom. Your fiancée has been trying to achieve some balance in this circus act for years, and now it's your turn to jump in the ring. The engagement period in particular might be difficult because it's fraught with so many possibilities—and so many opportunities for disagreement. If disagreement is the cornerstone of your future parents-in-law's relationship, beware. Your best bet is to steer clear of the overt dysfunction and leave the challenging communications to your fiancée. She already knows the rules. But you can help her by providing an empathetic ear if things get too crazy, both during the engagement period and after you're married.

Preparing for Major Life Changes

You knew getting into this engagement that marriage means change. Otherwise, you wouldn't have avoided it for so long. But what, exactly, is in store? Chapter 10, "Post-Marital Bliss and Blues: Creating a Home," outlines in detail some of the more practical changes, such as merging two homes and two bank accounts, with some tips to mastering both. But on a deeper level, the major changes are those of an emotional nature, such as being responsible to another person, having someone else rely on you, and creating a relationship and team that can weather the years.

As we are told again and again, marriage is not a commitment to be taken lightly. Fifty percent of marriages end in divorce—and the worst victims of this statistic are the children of these separated families. It's important to realize the gravity of what you are about to undertake and find the knowledge that it takes work to survive and thrive. That's what all the communication strategies are about. And if they don't work for you, by all means seek out some that do. Any problem can be solved by two willing participants and the right communication skills; that's pretty much what marriage is all about.

Groom Gambit

All it takes to solve a problem are two people willing to solve it, and two minds that are open enough to consider another option. Sometimes conflicts are even good for a relationship—their resolution can make a couple stronger.

Chapter 6

Pre-Wedding Events

In This Chapter

➤ The engagement party

➤ Bridal showers

➤ How to register for gifts, and why you might like it

➤ The rehearsal and dinner

➤ The politics of bachelor parties

In the days from your engagement leading up to your wedding, you are the star. There will probably be more than one party that revolves around you—yes, you—in the time preceding your wedding, where you will be charged with charming Great Aunt Molly, proving yourself to daddy, and graciously accepting blenders and other gifts you don't much care about. This is all part of the cult of wedding. Again, gender gaps are closing, so you might even be expected to attend a shower—unheard of in our parents' generation—and help your bride register. We're here to tell you what to expect, how to make the best of it—and maybe even have fun in the process.

The Engagement Party

Not every couple has or is expected to have an engagement party, but just in case you do, here's some information. Traditionally, the engagement party is thrown by the parents of the groom or the parents of the bride. However, anyone can throw an engagement party, including a sibling, a favorite uncle, a co-worker, a friend—even the two of you as a couple. If you do decide to throw one for yourselves, be sure it's clear you do not expect guests to bring gifts; you are inviting them for their good company and well wishes, not material items. If you are honored at an engagement party thrown by a friend or family, however, chances are good some guests will bring gifts, unless "No gifts" is specified on the invitation. In the event you will be receiving gifts, be sure to register ahead of time. (See more on that subject later in this chapter.)

The engagement party was traditionally thrown to introduce the new couple to friends and relatives of the family. If you've been dating for a number of years, you probably already know most of them; if so, consider yourself lucky. The party will be a lot easier if you're not meeting a large clan of unfamiliar people all at one time. If you are meeting a large clan of unknowns, though, you must adopt the attitude you'd take to a job interview: Make sure you're properly showered, shaved, and pressed, and don't say anything too stupid. You will be judged for many years according to your behavior on this day. Make it work for you, not against you. Be gracious and charming, and you will reap great rewards.

On engagement gifts—be sure to send out speedy thank-you notes acknowledging that you received and appreciated the generous gifts. And don't expect a gift, even if you are not throwing the party yourselves; engagement gifts are optional and should be received—or not received—with equal grace and aplomb.

Bridal Showers

Once strictly estrogen-only territory, showers, like weddings themselves, are evolving. Showers have traditionally been held to establish young couples emerging from their parents' homes with the household items they need to begin their new lives together. The bride would receive such gifts as china, silver, linens, and kitchen appliances—everything necessary to establish a working household.

Today's showers remain for much the same purpose, but occasionally feature a new twist: With brides and grooms getting married later, many engaged couples already have two households' full of things to merge. The last thing some couples need is a third coffee maker or toaster oven. As a result, some couples' well-wishers throw showers centered on a theme, such as home improvement, where couples then register at Home Depot for items to fix up their house or apartment. At a party for a honeymoon fund, guests can contribute money to a fund coordinated by the travel agent. Even sports can be the theme; avid skiers receive ski equipment, ski passes, or ski wear. Basically, the options are endless, although you probably will still, somewhere down the line, receive another toaster.

The other trend that you may or may not appreciate is the emergence of coed showers. Yes, you may be expected to attend this gathering formerly only the province of women, where you must eat crudités, drink punch and wine, and open gift after gift in front of a large group of people intent on your happy reactions to their particular offerings. Sound like fun? Just keep in mind that you're probably having more fun than your father who's also forced to be there; at least you get something to take home at the end of the night.

Groom Gambit

If you are given a coed shower, you will be expected to join your future bride in opening gifts. Be sure to be gracious, thanking each gift-giver individually by name and if possible making a personal comment about the gift, such as, "This wok will be terrific when I cook my wife dinner after a long day." In other words, it's a great suck-up opportunity.

Actually, if approached the right way, coed showers can be a lot of fun; your friends are there, her friends are there, and your family rounds out the group. These showers have been known to turn into full-scale parties similar to an engagement party, with good food and spirits paving the way.

Collecting the Loot

As mentioned earlier in this chapter, you will be receiving a great number of gifts during your engagement and up to a year after your wedding. This is a perk of weddings that you may have forgotten. If your idea of an exciting gift is not a blender, do not forget that household items can also include such choices as a stereo, an espresso maker, a DVD player...do I have your interest yet? In other words, it's up to you and your bride what kind of loot you'll be *registering* for.

Wedding Words

Registering is the process of creating a "wish list" of household items you'd like to receive as wedding and shower gifts, through a department or specialty store or both. Registering makes guests' choices of gifts easy and guarantees that you'll receive the items you need in the right quantities.

If you think registering for your wedding is akin to asking people for gifts, you're right. However, this is the one time that formal etiquette allows—even promotes—such overt greediness. In reality, registering for gifts actually saves your guests much time and anxiety over choosing a gift; it provides an organized way for couples to receive the gifts they really need, without duplication. Your guests are going to give you a gift anyway; why not make it something that you actually need and that your guests will be confident you'll appreciate?

There are a few rules to registering:

Rule #1: First, you can register in more than one place; in fact, that's probably the preferable way to do things if you are having a medium- to large-sized wedding. With multiple registrations, your guests will have a choice about where they can purchase your gift so they can pursue the most convenient option. You can register at stores ranging from Tiffany to Target, with department stores and specialty stores such as Pier One and Pottery Barn in between. Shop around a bit before you decide where you definitely want to register.

Rule #2: Be sure to register for gifts in different price ranges. Not all your guests want to buy you a $100 place setting for a shower gift, and there are only a handful of guests who will be spending enough on your wedding gift to afford the DVD player. Make sure you have enough lower-priced items to balance your list, even if guests feel the need to buy you three smaller gifts.

Rule #3: Timing is everything. If you're having an engagement that lasts longer than year, a good rule of thumb is to wait at least six months before registering (unless you are having a major party such as a shower or engagement party before that). The reason you should wait is that store inventory changes, and you don't want to start a set of crystal glasses or china that the store will discontinue carrying in eight months.

But don't wait too long; as mentioned previously, you want to register before you have any major parties so guests have more options and you can begin receiving gifts based on exactly what you want and need.

Nuptial No-Nos

Don't register for more than your guest list can handle; consult a sales associate to determine the proper number of items and price ranges to choose from. You don't want to end up with half the number of place settings, silver, or glassware that you've registered for, unless you want to cough up a generous chunk of cash to finish off the list.

Rule #4: You don't have to register for the traditional china, crystal, and linens that your parents registered for.

Couples are choosing all sorts of creative options, such as registries at Home Depot, sporting goods stores, and Target for more practical items they don't have and really want or need. If you've already got two sets of dishes, glassware, and silverware, why not register for a barbecue grill or lawnmower—two items on the more practical side you may need down the line? Or register for furniture: One guest doesn't have to purchase the whole thing. Rather, multiple guests can contribute to a fund that adds up to the total price. Check with your favorite stores to learn their specific policies and advice regarding non-traditional registering. Remember, it doesn't hurt to ask any store to set up a registry for you, even if they don't regularly offer this service. After all, you're bringing them some serious business for the small amount of time it'll take to set you up.

Rule #5: It is proper to include registry information in the shower invitation, but not in the wedding invitation. Rely on friends and relatives to spread the word about where you're registered for wedding gifts.

Many stores will offer you a one-year discount following your wedding to purchase any remaining items on your registry, so you can complete unfinished sets of dishes, glasses, appliances, and cookware that you've received. Many stores will keep your information on hand for at least a year so that procrastinating guests can still consult it up to the etiquette-inspired year's deadline they have to buy you a wedding gift.

The following are the traditional lists of items couples use as a gift registry guide. Remember, it's fine to stray off the list, but don't forget that the china that seems overly expensive and impractical now will become a necessary evil when you start entertaining friends, family, and business associates in the not-so-distant future.

Tableware (8 to 12 five-piece formal place settings):

- ➤ Dinner plate
- ➤ Bread-and-butter plate
- ➤ Saucer
- ➤ Salad/dessert plate
- ➤ Cup

You might also want to order a casual or transitional pattern to be dressed up or down in addition to your formal china.

Additional tableware pieces:

- ➤ Platter
- ➤ Gravy boat
- ➤ Salt and pepper shakers
- ➤ Vegetable bowls
- ➤ Sugar bowl and creamer

Glassware (same quantity as dinnerware):

- ➤ Goblets
- ➤ All-purpose wine glasses
- ➤ Double old-fashioned glasses
- ➤ Iced-beverage glasses
- ➤ Champagne flutes

Flatware (same quantity as dinnerware):

- ➤ Dinner fork
- ➤ Soup spoon
- ➤ Tea/dessert spoon
- ➤ Dinner knife
- ➤ Salad/dessert fork

You can choose from sterling, silver plate, and stainless steel. You might want to register for two sets—formal and casual.

Additional pieces of flatware:

- ➤ Hostess set
- ➤ Extra teaspoons
- ➤ Salad serving set
- ➤ Extra salad forks

Cookware (register for boxed sets or individual pieces):

➤ 10" frying pan or skillet

➤ Eight-quart stockpot

➤ Grill or griddle

➤ Two-quart and three-quart saucepans

➤ Roasting pan

If you fancy yourself somewhat of a gourmet, you'll probably want to register for high quality pots and pans. Copper pans are best for equal heat distribution.

Linens: Bedroom

➤ Three sets of sheets

➤ Three sets of pillowcases

➤ Comforter and duvet

➤ Bed skirt

➤ Pillows

➤ Blankets

Linens: Bathroom

➤ Two sets of hand towels per bathroom

➤ Two sets of face towels per bathroom

➤ Two sets of bath towels per bathroom

➤ Shower curtains

➤ Bath mats

➤ Guest towels

Linens: Kitchen

➤ Two to four sets of table linens—one formal in damask, lace, or linen

➤ Place mats and napkins

Choose colors, patterns, and fabrics that will mix and match. You may want to let your bride coordinate colors for linens. If you're not sure about a color scheme for your house yet, choose neutral colors.

Kitchenware:

- ➤ Blender
- ➤ Slow cooker
- ➤ Food processor
- ➤ Toaster or toaster oven
- ➤ Bread maker
- ➤ Coffee maker
- ➤ Electric can opener
- ➤ Hand mixer
- ➤ Microwave

Cutlery:

- ➤ 8" chef's knife
- ➤ Paring knife
- ➤ Sharpening steel
- ➤ Knife block to hold them all
- ➤ Bread knife
- ➤ Utility knife
- ➤ Pair of kitchen shears
- ➤ 8 to 12 steak knives

Additional items:

- ➤ Garlic press
- ➤ Spatulas
- ➤ Measuring cups and spoons
- ➤ Mixing spoons
- ➤ Cheese grater
- ➤ Vegetable peeler

Here are some ideas beyond the basics:

- ➤ Electronics, including a fax machine, an alarm clock, or a CD player
- ➤ Giftware, including vases, picture frames, and candlesticks
- ➤ Necessities for the home, including an iron, ironing board, smoke alarm, or shower massage.

For the basics, these items should have you covered. For more guidance, make an appointment with your favorite department or specialty store, where a sales associate will assist you in coordinating patterns and tailoring your list to the number of guests.

Rehearsal Dinner

Another of the pre-wedding events, the rehearsal dinner is typically held one to two days before the wedding. The rehearsal dinner usually follows the ceremony rehearsal, where the bride, groom, bridesmaids, groomsmen, and other honored participants are coached on the proceedings of the ceremony so they won't screw up too badly during the main event. The dinner that follows is traditionally thrown by the groom's family, but as with the wedding expenses, the cost can be split according to your individual situation.

The dinner can be anything from a formal sit-down meal to a more casual, backyard-type affair, depending on your preferences and what your parents have in mind. If you'd like, this is the one area where you can really get involved, in light of the fact that your parents are those planning it (or perhaps you're doing it yourself). In any event, the rehearsal dinner is a big part of the wedding festivities and can often be just as much fun—if not more fun—than the actual wedding day, if only because it's a bit more intimate.

Groom Gambit

It is traditional to give your groomsmen a special gift for taking part in your wedding. Popular gifts include silver money clips, watches, silver or glass steins, and Swiss Army knives—basically something that will stand the test of time. The rehearsal dinner is the most popular time to present groomsmen with their gifts.

Invited to the rehearsal dinner should be the bride and groom; your parents; your siblings and their spouses or guests; your grandparents; the wedding party and ceremony participants and their spouses or guests; and optionally, any out of town guests. It is also nice to invite the clergy performing your ceremony, especially if he or she is a friend of the family.

It is customary for the bride and groom to say a few words at the rehearsal dinner, thanking their parents and guests for their love and support. Speeches may precede or follow dinner. Your father might also want to say a few words, as he is this evening's host. The floor is then open to anyone who wants to make a toast, including the best man, maid of honor, or other guests who want to honor the bride and groom.

Be careful not to stay out too late—or drink too much—if your rehearsal dinner is the night before the wedding. It'll probably be tempting; you'll be excited and maybe a little nervous, and all your friends and close family will want to celebrate with you, too. Just keep in mind that the next day is one of the most important in your life. You want to be well-rested and clear-headed.

The Bachelor Party (a.k.a. How Much Do I Love My Bride?)

Chances are, you've already been to a few bachelor parties and you are already well aware of the chain of events— liquor, gambling, and the requisite dancing girls, not necessarily in that order. The object of this night is, ultimately, to abuse such vices in pursuit of some unnamed or unidentified goal, resulting in behavior you wouldn't be proud of if your mother found out.

For whatever reason, men revel in this sort of excess. Pre-marriage, it is the ultimate exercise in independence, proving once and for all that a man can still do what a man wants to do. In this spirit, you might end up offending your bride; tread carefully during this sensitive time right before the wedding. Women today know exactly what can happen at these parties, so if you must take part in activities of which she would not approve, keep it as tame and respectful as possible. One exercise to help put it all in perspective is imagining your bride out with her girlfriends, picking up some Ricky Martin look-a-like with whom she ends up entangled before coming home to you. Probably not on your top-10 list of favorite images.

Aside from their bad rap among the female population, there are plenty of worthwhile activities surrounding the bachelor party, including spending quality time with a large group of friends (or a small group, depending on your preference). Renting out a bar for a few hours of gambling and raising money for the groom is one popular option, as is a day of golf or sailing or a night on the town with the guys. Anything where her father would be comfortable is known as a "gentleman's bachelor party"; that is, you're doing nothing to make him feel he should start cleaning his gun collection anytime soon.

Word to the wise: If you can't stand the heat, get out of the kitchen. Post-bachelor party residue can get ugly, so the key is being honest and respectful. The rest is up to you.

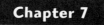

Chapter 7

Finally the Good Stuff: Honeymoon Planning

In This Chapter

➤ Types of honeymoons

➤ The honeymoon planner

➤ Popular honeymoon destinations

➤ Preparing and packing

For most men, planning a honeymoon invokes one of two reactions—great anticipation or serious dread. After all, this might be the first real trip you need to plan—somewhat different from the usual wake up, pack, gas up the car, and hope it gets you to your buddy's place in New York City/San Francisco/Chicago without breaking down. If you haven't been on an extended trip with your fiancée yet, here is one great truth you will soon learn: Traveling with women is very different. Women are more organized. Women are more rigid. Women plan what to pack weeks in advance so they can go shopping.

If you follow traditional etiquette, you, as the groom, are charged with planning this Cadillac of all trips. With an endless number of destinations and potential activities, this is a heady responsibility. You will need a structured plan to follow to ensure that you and your bride will end up with a room to sleep in and some things to do during the day—or at the very least, gas in your car.

Types of Honeymoons

So there's a world of destination possibilities and you've barely been across state lines. A honeymoon is your one great excuse to be extravagant—to go somewhere you've never gone, spend more cash on a hotel than you could ever justify another time, and do something totally impractical. With all these options, where's a guy to start? The following checklist will help you narrow down the unlimited options you face so you can start thinking seriously about where you're going to end up.

Check the top three most interesting or important activities for you and your bride on your honeymoon:

- ❏ Relaxing on a beach
- ❏ Casino gambling
- ❏ Golfing
- ❏ Playing water sports
- ❏ Playing tennis
- ❏ Skiing
- ❏ Trying adventure sports (whitewater rafting, mountain climbing, and so on)
- ❏ Seeing a new city
- ❏ Touring a number of cities
- ❏ Touring museums
- ❏ Touring art galleries

- ❏ Touring historical sites
- ❏ Touring natural wonders (volcanoes, waterfalls, and so on)
- ❏ Shopping
- ❏ Fine dining
- ❏ Exploring a new culture
- ❏ Backpacking
- ❏ Experiencing great nightlife
- ❏ Getting away from it all
- ❏ Pampering from a spa
- ❏ Attending special events (Olympics, bullfighting, Mardi Gras, Tour de France, and so on)

Once you've chosen your top three interests, it becomes much easier to narrow down your options. For instance, if you've chosen gambling, beaches, and great nightlife, there's Aruba or Monte Carlo. If you've chosen fine dining, shopping, and museums, any cosmopolitan city in the world will do, from Paris to Sydney to Rio to New York. Got the idea? Once you have an idea of the type of vacation you want, you'll be able to pick and choose your destination based on budgetary, timing, and travel considerations.

Your next step is to consult a travel agent, who will have a lot of ideas about where your interests can be found. Ask around for references to a good travel agent. If you are a real do-it-yourselfer, begin researching online or in the travel section of your local bookstore. See Appendix B, "Wedding Resources," for some starting points.

Groom Gambit

Your options are unlimited when it comes to the types of activities for your honeymoon. Provided that your bride is game, you can make a beach getaway, sightsee in Europe, join an African safari, or hike Antarctica. This is one vacation where you'll feel justified being a little extravagant.

Honeymoon Planner

It's always easier to plan with a timeline. The following lists will take you from six months before your vacation to the day before you leave so you won't forget any important honeymoon details:

At least six months in advance:

➤ Investigate possible destinations. Use the preceding checklist and then consult with a travel agent, friends and family, and the Internet for options and referrals.

➤ Reserve airline tickets and get a confirmation number.

➤ Reserve hotels and specify the type of room (smoking, beachfront, and so on).

➤ Reserve a rental car and get a confirmation number.

➤ Sign up for foreign language classes or buy tapes if you're going abroad.

Three months in advance:

➤ Obtain passports.

➤ Finalize all reservations.

Two months ahead:

➤ Make a shopping list of items you'll need for the trip (such as film, batteries, and an adapter if traveling abroad).

➤ Get the proper vaccinations.

One month ahead:

➤ Confirm all reservations.

➤ Order special meals from the airlines.

➤ Book tours, tee times, theater tickets, massages, dinners, and other activities that require reservations through your travel agent, tour operator, or hotel concierge.

➤ Make arrangements for dog- or cat-sitting, plant watering, or house-sitting.

➤ Get any prescriptions or medications you can't do without.

Two weeks ahead:

➤ Pick up tickets, boarding passes, transfers, and vouchers from the travel agent.

➤ Buy travelers' checks, and copy the numbers of checks in case they're lost or stolen.

One week ahead:

➤ Arrange to have mail held at the post office or ask someone to pick it up.

➤ Stop newspaper delivery; a pile of newspapers on your doorstep is a thief's welcome mat.

➤ Ask the stores where you've registered to temporarily stop deliveries, or arrange for someone to pick up gifts.

➤ Begin packing.

➤ Organize addresses to write thank-you notes on the plane.

Three days ahead:

➤ Reconfirm overseas flights.

➤ Buy books or magazines for the plane and poolside.

➤ Arrange transportation to and from the airport.

➤ Leave your itinerary with a relative in case of emergency.

➤ Check the weather reports for your destination.

One day ahead:

➤ Reconfirm domestic flights.

➤ Get your house ready for departure: Take out the garbage, clean out the fridge, set timers, and so on.

Nuptial No-No

Don't forget to pay the bills that will be due while you're away, especially if you're going on an extended honeymoon. Also, check your credit card balances before you leave to be sure there's plenty of room for honeymoon indulgences—or emergencies.

Popular Honeymoon Destinations

Back in the day, Niagara Falls was the king of honeymoon destinations, with thousands of honeymooners and celebrities visiting every year. The Falls are still there, but the romance has been replaced by wax museums, The Hard Rock Cafe, Planet Hollywood, and a great big casino. A sign of the times, perhaps....

In our mobile society, today's honeymooners are more likely to travel outside the United States, from the Caribbean to Europe to the South Pacific. Smart resorts now market themselves to extravagance-prone honeymooners and cater to couples once they arrive. The following sections, while by no means a comprehensive list, describe some of today's hot honeymoon destinations.

The Caribbean

With a seemingly endless list of islands to choose from, the Caribbean has a lot to offer for those seeking a beach honeymoon with any number of variations, such as golf, water sports, gambling, sightseeing, shopping, and nightlife. There seems to be an island for every couple, depending on your priorities. For secluded beaches, gorgeous gardens, and a slightly formal atmosphere, visit Bermuda. St. Lucia offers the natural beauty of mountains, rain forests, and a more rustic feel, with West Indian culture. Aruba is known for its spectacular blue water, great beaches, and glittering casinos. Jamaica, one of the largest islands, has a host of options, including many *all-inclusive resorts*.

Wedding Words

An **all-inclusive resort** offers a pay-one-price package deal that includes such amenities as airfare, accommodations, meals, drinks, and sports and activities. Be sure to verify the details. The beauty of all-inclusives is that there are no hidden costs; you don't have to think about money once you're there, even for tipping. Popular resorts include Sandals, Super Clubs, Breezes, Couples, and Club Med.

Hawaii

Hawaii is arguably the most popular honeymoon destination for American newlyweds. Travel agents credit the romantic atmosphere, laid-back environment, beautiful natural surroundings, endless stretches of beaches, and island history to Hawaii's never-ending draw of tourists.

Hawaii's attractions are split among the six islands, which include Maui, Kauai, The Big Island, Oahu, Lanai, and Mookai. Maui is the most popular honeymoon spot, with its great beaches, diving, and activities such as biking, water sports, and helicopter rides. There are some beautiful Maui resorts both near the center of the action and farther away from it; you can take your pick.

Kauai's lush natural beauty is marked by gorgeous waterfalls, cliffs, and sea caves. The Big Island is great for couples interested in sightseeing, golfing, and volcano-hiking. For couples seeking a lot of activity, Oahu is home to Waikiki Beach, which is swarming with restaurants, nightlife, and surfers from around the world. There are plenty of other activities as well, including kayaking, hiking, and traditional games and crafts.

Groom Gambit

Don't miss one of Hawaii's traditional luaus. A luau, if you'll recall, is a beach party like the one attended by the Brady family at the end of their big Hawaiian trip (after Greg, Peter, and Bobby got rid of the cursed Tiki, of course). Luaus are filled with great food, music, and dancing—particularly that of a belly nature, wink, wink.

For those seeking more seclusion, Hawaii's islands of Lanai or Molokai are true getaways. They are both secluded and dedicated to preserving their natural resources. Lanai is mostly rugged terrain, with only two ultra-upscale hotels.

Europe

There are so many worthwhile destinations in Europe that it's difficult to go into detail on any few of them. But here goes: If you're seeking history and culture, including museums, galleries, and architecture, why not try London, Paris, Madrid, Berlin, Amsterdam, Athens, Rome, or Venice? The list goes on and on. To narrow it down, why not travel to your ancestors' homelands? If you're Italian and she's Irish, travel to both countries to infuse more meaning into your honeymoon. If you'd like to experience the most number of cities in the least amount of time, buy Eurail passes and travel from country to country. If you decide to do a bit of traveling, be sure to establish an itinerary ahead of time so that you get the accommodations that you desire in each city. There's nothing worse than scrounging around for vacancies when you're dead tired and you just want to relax, especially in a foreign country.

If you're seeking Europe by seaside, you've still got a lot of options, such as the French Riviera and Monaco, Estoril, Portugal, Italy's Amalfi coast, and Barcelona, Spain. These destinations also offer big-city attractions such as fine restaurants and sightseeing.

French Polynesia

The islands of Tahiti and Bora Bora in the South Pacific are a honeymooner's dream. Although it'll take you some time to get there (you're flying literally halfway around the world), tourists say it's worth the trip. You might want to extend your honeymoon by a few days if you travel this far, however, to get over jet lag and to have enough time to kick back and relax.

The islands are exotic and romantic, and offer fantastic diving and gorgeous beaches. Their spectacular scenery includes mountains, tropical rainforests, and quaint South Seas ports. Affordable package deals are available, especially if you choose to island hop; check with a travel agent for the best deals.

The Good Old U.S. of A.

Many honeymooners overlook the host of options available here in the U.S. There are plenty of great destinations for honeymooners, including such diverse options as South Beach in Miami, an art-deco cosmopolitan beach community infected with non-stop nightlife and hordes of beautiful people. Or why not drive the Pacific Coast Highway and splurge on fabulous hotels along the way in Malibu, Carmel, and Beverly Hills? Or you could try Savannah or Charleston, cities rich with history and old southern charm? Then there's New York City, the tourist mecca, with its endless attractions and world-renowned restaurants, hotels, and shopping. A few more options to consider: Lake Tahoe, stretching the borders of Nevada and California; the Poconos in Pennsylvania; Colorado for adventure sports and skiing; Arizona for top golf; Hilton Head Island off the coast of South Carolina for golf and tennis; or New Orleans for sightseeing, culture, and revelry. Check with friends, relatives, and a travel agent for more options.

Cruises

Cruises are a great way to experience many ports of call with minimal worry about travel or finances. Their all-inclusive nature appeals to honeymooners who want to pay up-front for a worry-free vacation. Cruises are well-regarded for their top-of-the-line unlimited menus—some cruises even offer 24-hour dining—and diverse entertainment, all included in one price. You can find great deals on cruises with two-for-one options and free room upgrades, if you keep your eyes open. Cruises are popular among honeymooners, so chances are you'll meet other couples in the same boat (no pun intended). Cruises also known to pamper guests, especially honeymooners.

The most popular cruises travel among the Caribbean islands, Mexico, and the Bahamas. But cruises are now developing itineraries that include destinations in Alaska, the Greek Islands, Turkey, and the South Pacific. Some cruises stop at private islands for water sports and other activities.

Groom Gambit

To get the biggest bang for your cruise buck, you can follow a few strategies. Book early to get the best deal; get your specific room request guaranteed (such as an outside cabin); and be flexible about your vacation priorities. If you want the best room, you might have to forgo booking on the newest ship.

Consult with a travel agent before booking a cruise, or do some homework yourself on the Internet. All cruises are not created equal, so be sure to get referrals from people you trust before booking. Some of the more popular and reputable cruise lines include Royal Caribbean, Carnival, Princess Cruises, Celebrity Cruises, and Holland America. There are many more, so be sure to check with your travel agent for other options.

If you've got an unlimited budget, you can have a truly unforgettable cruise. Luxury ships offer personalized service and amenities to match their price tags. Upscale cabins offer such extras as private balconies, private Jacuzzis, or king-sized beds. Romantic destinations such as Europe, the South Pacific, and the Orient can make a mediocre cruise shine. The motto of cruises? If you want it, it's out there.

The drawback of cruises is that your options are somewhat limited by the ever-moving nature of the cruise; you might be able to spend only a few hours in ports where you'd like to stay longer. You are also assigned a table for dinner for the duration of the cruise—so if you get stuck with irritating people, you're in for some long, potentially annoying meals.

How to Pack

So you've chosen your destination, you're following your planning timeline to a "T," and now it's time to pack. Unless you've gone to military school, chances are you're a sloppy packer. Most men are; it's a metaphor for why we get married, really. In the event that your wife-to-be is not yet packing for you, here are some sure-fire tips for packing that you'll bring to your honeymoon and beyond:

➤ Pack in advance. Waiting until the last minute only causes stress when you realize that many of your clothing favorites are rumpled, stained, or missing. Packing in advance leaves time for laundry and shopping for the few items you might need, such as new swim trunks, sunglasses, or ski poles.

➤ Check the weather predictions for your destination a day in advance, in case any unexpected climate changes are blowing through the area.

> Bring necessities from home, such as sunscreen, medications, and especially prescriptions. If you're in a foreign country, you might not be able to get the types you need.

> Pack toiletries that could leak in a plastic bag. There's nothing worse than arriving at your destination with a bag full of clothing covered in hair gel or shampoo.

> Carry valuables or one-of-a-kind items such as glasses or jewelry in your carry-on bag. You just never know when a bag could end up in airline limbo.

> Make sure you label all luggage. It'll save you a lot of grief if your luggage is somehow routed to the wrong destination.

> Pack enough, but pack lightly. You'll want some room left for honeymoon souvenirs!

Groom Gambit

Why not surprise your bride with a honeymoon destination? Just give her a little advance notice on the honeymoon climate so she can shop and pack the appropriate wardrobe.

If it's not clear by now, the key to all of this honeymoon planning is preparation. The more that's left to chance, the more plans that can go awry. A little extra legwork now will almost guarantee a relaxing, painless vacation later.

Chapter 8

Guy Stuff

In This Chapter

➤ Choosing the right formalwear

➤ How to get a marriage license

➤ Picking out a wedding ring

➤ Gift ideas for your bride

The details are planned and the countdown has begun. You're either relieved or starting to sweat more by the day. No matter how little or how much you've already been involved in this process, a few additional considerations will require a bit of thought on your part—unless you want to set the ultimate precedent for this union, sucking out any independent thought for life. You'll definitely want input into such decisions as your formalwear and your wedding ring; after all, what you're wearing is the ultimate reflection of your personality and style. And when it comes to choosing a gift for her (no, you weren't off the hook with the engagement ring), you'll want to give a gift she will keep and cherish always. This chapter is meant to guide you in these murky decision-making waters—so you don't look all washed up.

Puttin' on the Ritz

Even if your wedding is casual, you should put some serious thought into what you choose to wear on your wedding day. A few immediate tips:

1. Don't wear something you even remotely think you'll cringe upon seeing in 20 years.

2. Don't choose something just because it's outrageous, even if your typical modus operandi is less than conservative. Your wedding day is a serious event, and your clothing should reflect that gravity.

3. Choose something classic that fits well and reflects your taste. If your bride is steering you to wear something you just won't feel comfortable in (such as a loud cummerbund or top hat and tails), then change direction and choose what you want. This is your wedding day too, don't forget.

Groom Gambit

Some men eschew the formal tuxedo altogether. One groom chose a well-cut suit for his wedding and subsidized matching suits for his groomsmen. Three years later, former groomsmen are still being spotted around town in their well-worn wedding suits—making the money that would have gone toward a one-time tux rental a great investment.

On your wedding day, you want to make a statement. Your statement, mind you, should speak volumes in its style and subtlety. Your wedding, I regret to inform you, is not the ideal place to don your Disney characters bow tie and vest. Nor is it the time to go on the cheap. If you're renting, as the majority of men do, spend a little extra on the style, colors, and fabrics that best suit you. Or take this opportunity to finally purchase a tuxedo, especially if you have a more active formal social calendar. To women, a well-made, tailored-to-fit tuxedo is akin to a thong bathing suit from a man's perspective; it turns heads. Just look at James Bond's success with the ladies.

Whether you're renting or buying, you have many styles to choose from. Here's a crash course in formalwear to get the ball rolling.

Jacket Styles

➤ **Single-breasted.** This jacket has one row of buttons down the front. Single-breasted jackets come with one-, two-, three-, and four-button styles, so choose the style that you like best. Generally, the more buttons you choose, the taller and narrower you should be for it to flatter. Barrel-chested or stout men might look a bit like stuffed sausage in higher-buttoned jackets.

➤ **Double-breasted.** David Letterman's signature jacket. Traditionally, they're a bit boxy, but in recent years, shaped double-breasted jackets have become the trend. Any body type can look good in this style—and it can be an especially good one to choose if you want to hide a few extra beers.

➤ **Tails.** Highly formal, this jacket is characterized by its short-in-front, long-in-back design—kinda like your high school hair style. Short, stout men might want to steer clear of this style, which can make them look like a penguin.

➤ **Cutaway.** A.K.A. morning coat. Looking good on just about any frame, this jacket tapers from the waistline button to one broad tail in the back, with a vent. Very Kennedy. Very Hollywood.

➤ **Dinner jacket.** Single- or double-breasted jacket in white, ivory, or novelty fabrics worn with black, satin-striped trousers.

Single Breasted
(one button)

Single Breasted
(three button)

Double Breasted
(two button)

Double Breasted
(six button)

Variation of Double
Breasted (six button)

Full Dress (tail coat)

Cutaway

Notch Lapel

Peak Lapel

Shawl Lapel

Wing Collar

Banded Collar

Laydown Collar

Other Formalwear Basics

The jacket style you choose helps dictate your other formalwear options, including vests, trousers, and neckwear. For instance, if you choose a cutaway coat, you should choose a low vest and ascot for the classic look you're trying to achieve. But if you choose a single- or double-breasted jacket, your options are more versatile:

Groom Gambit

Have each of your attendants get his formalwear properly fitted ahead of time in case there are any problems. The sooner any mishaps are detected, the more time you'll have to solve the problem.

➤ **High vest.** Vests are where you can really express your individuality. High vests look best on taller, narrower men. If you're very broad-chested, choose a vest that's muted, not too bright.

➤ **Low vest.** Generally, these look good on all men, except in the cases where they can look like belly slings. Large beer bellies should steer clear.

➤ **Bow tie.** You wore a clip-on to the prom. This time, choose one you have to tie yourself.

➤ **Four-in-hand tie.** Very now. This knotted tie hangs vertically, like a business-suit tie. It should be worn with a spread collar (business-shirt collar).

➤ **Ascot.** Very society. Broad neck scarf looped under the chin, fastened with a tie tack or stick pin, and worn with a wing collar.

➤ **Wing collar.** Collar with downward points; looks great with an ascot or bow tie.

➤ **Laydown collar.** Similar to a business shirt collar.

➤ **Mandarin or banded collar.** Think priest's collar crossed with Euro style. No tie is worn. Avoid this if you've got a thick, short, or heavy neck.

Unless you regularly read *GQ* and know the definition of "couture," you may also want your bride's input as to the most flattering and appropriate style for your wedding.

Formalwear Sizing

An ill-fitting tuxedo is one of the sadder things in life. The implication is that you care enough to don some serious formalwear but that you have poor follow-through. Or worse, it's a cheap rental. Maybe some other time, you can get away with it. But on your wedding day, honor the occasion with a tux that fits well. Here are a few tips to make sure you're in good shape:

➤ Make sure the store has a tailor on the premises. If pant legs don't fit, they can be hemmed or let out in 10 minutes. If not, ask the store in advance whether it has an affiliation with a tailor for last-minute alterations.

➤ If you're renting, pick up your tux as early as possible—preferably a day or two in advance. That way, the store will have more time to fix any problems.

➤ Shirts should hug the neck and be neither too loose nor too tight.

➤ Pants should touch the top of shoes.

➤ Waistbands are often adjustable; check for side buckles.

➤ Jacket should fit snugly but comfortably around shoulders, with no arm bulges and some room at the waist.

➤ Collar should hug the neck and lapels shouldn't buckle.

➤ Jackets sleeves should end at the wrist bone.

> ### Nuptial No-No
>
> Don't forget to return any rented formalwear after your wedding; you can be charged by the day for late returns. If you are leaving for your honeymoon immediately following the wedding, appoint a (trusted) groomsman—or ask your father—to return yours when he returns his own.

Making It Legal

Before you are officially bound by the ties of marriage, it's necessary to make the proper legal arrangements. That means you must secure a wedding license in advance—but not too far in advance because marriage licenses expire after a relatively short period of time. Unless you're getting married in Las Vegas, where instant wedding licenses are de rigeur, you should get it far enough in advance to bridge any waiting period dictates. Every state in the union has different laws in place; in New York, for example, there's no waiting period, but your license will expire after 60 days. In South Dakota, it'll expire after only 20. Check your local laws to be sure you're legally intact for the big day.

To get a license in most states, the bride and groom must show up in person at the county courthouse. You will be asked for current photo IDs and certified or notarized copies of birth certificates. If either party is divorced, you might need to bring a copy of the divorce degree or annulment; if one of you is widowed, a death certificate may be required. Call your local county courthouse in advance to determine exactly what you'll need so you don't have to make another trip. (Or endure questions from your betrothed like "Why didn't you call them in advance, stupid?")

You will need to protect this license beyond your wedding day. If you are traveling out of the country or even just by plane, and you have booked your tickets as "Mr. and Mrs. Groom," you might need some sort of proof that your wife is now "Mrs. Groom"—beyond, of course, your googly-eyed, newlywed affection at the airport counter.

With This Ring

If you thought your jewelry-buying days were over once you scored the engagement ring, think again. Not only do you have to buy her another ring, but you'll also have to pick one out for yourself. If you're not the jewelry-wearing type, the thought of wearing a ring might turn you off at first. But don't be surprised if your bride feels it's pretty important that you keep it on. After all, the ring is a symbol of one of the most important commitments you make in your lifetime. She figures you should both declare your marital status to the world.

We know of one young gentleman who really hated wearing his wedding ring. Not only did the aesthetics offend him, but he also claimed it was uncomfortable and that exceptionally hearty handshakes actually hurt. So he decided to take matters into his own hands. He hid the ring in the pocket of an old pair of pants he never wore and told his bride, with a hangdog expression, that someone must have stolen it from his locker at the gym. He felt just terrible about it, he said. Although she wasn't pleased, she understood that such things happen, and they didn't replace it right away because of a temporary cash-flow issue. Six months later, while going through clothes to donate to the Salvation Army, she found the ring. The ensuing scene was not pretty. And that ring has not come off his hand since. Not for sports. Not for swimming. Not for anything.

The moral? Don't be sneaky. You'll get more leeway on the ring issue, and many more like it, if you approach the conflict more directly.

Okay, now that we've established that you've got to wear a ring, what type of ring will you choose? There are many more variations today than just the traditional plain band of gold. Some men choose white gold or platinum to match their brides' engagement and wedding rings. Some men choose rings with subtle patterns or cuts, which can add a more interesting flair. Also popular now are rings with two metals, such as yellow and white gold or yellow gold and platinum.

Etiquette dictates that your bride purchase your wedding ring, but we know you'll probably want some input in choosing it. While you're at it, you should also choose a wedding ring for your bride, which you are responsible for purchasing. Your best bet is to consult with your original jeweler for a band style that will best complement the original engagement ring. Especially if you've given her a traditional band with a solitaire diamond as an engagement ring, you can really create a gorgeous combination with the addition of the wedding ring.

Obviously, the wedding rings are crucial to the wedding ceremony. Your best man should keep them close prior to the ceremony so that they are not forgotten on wedding day.

Gift Ideas for Your Bride

Just when you thought it was over—you bought the engagement ring and wedding ring and you are pitching in for the wedding expenses—you have to be told or reminded of another gift for the bride. What do you mean, another gift? Traditionally, the bride and groom exchange additional gifts for their wedding. Is this absolutely necessary? If you agree in advance not to exchange gifts, it's not absolutely necessary. But if you'd like to mark the occasion with another special remembrance, you might want to think about some of the following suggestions:

➤ Jewelry, especially jewelry she can wear on her wedding day. A lovely strand of pearls, pearl or sapphire earrings (something blue), a delicate platinum bracelet—anything goes. She will probably plan ahead what jewelry she's wearing on her wedding day, so you might want to give her your special gift a little early—or prep her that something might be on its way.

➤ Something related to a hobby. If she's an avid reader, find a limited, antique, or signed edition of a book by her favorite author. If she paints, get her the expensive brush set she's always wanted but has been too practical to splurge on. A skier might want a new pair of parabolic skis. Whatever her hobby, get her something that has thought behind it and something that will have lasting value.

➤ Something for the house. An original piece of artwork. An antique vanity table. A pretty window box for flowers. Heck, even a dishwasher. Basically anything that will add beauty and make her life easier.

➤ Giftware, such as a beautiful vase or clock from Tiffany's. Or a splurge item from her favorite specialty store.

➤ Luxurious, expensive lingerie that she would never buy for herself.

➤ Spa treatments.

➤ Tickets to a special vacation destination for your first anniversary.

➤ Something handmade or homemade. If you're a writer or artist, create something original honoring this day. If you're great with your hands, build a rocking chair or table. Plant her a garden that will bloom year after year. Originality and creativity are especially worthy here.

➤ Flower-of-the-month club. Online clubs and florists are marketing special plans where you can pre-order and pre-pay for flowers to arrive on your doorstep at regular intervals, such as every month for a year. Drop hints that you'd like the similarly designed beer-of-the-month membership.

➤ See Appendix C, "Gift-Giving Guide," for more ideas.

While all this fussing and detail work about clothing and gifts may not be your usual style, they *are* important and symbolic to your bride. Don't fight about this stuff—an enthusiastic attitude and a little extra time spent can go a long way, whether you're choosing just the right wedding band or looking for a special gift for your bride. And she, for one, will never forget it.

Chapter 9

I Hear Bells Ringing (Am I Hallucinating?)

> ### In This Chapter
>
> ➤ Pre-wedding activities to keep your mind occupied
> ➤ Tips for relieving wedding-related stress
> ➤ Surviving cold feet
> ➤ Writing your own vows
> ➤ Wedding-day traditions
> ➤ Wedding-day etiquette

You've pored over the plans for months, discerning the best strategies to make this operation go smoothly. You've endured conflicts with underlings, peers, and superiors in your quest to make things right. The only thing left to do is wait and watch and hope that the operation goes smoothly and that there are few wedding-day casualties. It's D-Day, Colonel Commitment; read ahead for some wedding-day operatives that'll earn you your stripes.

What Do I Do All Day?

If you're having a late afternoon wedding, you will quickly learn the meaning of the word anticipation. Even if you do little else on Saturdays besides sleep and watch MTV marathons of *The Real World,* you will find that having nothing to do before your wedding is excruciating. First of all, you can't count on your betrothed; she will have a lot of things to do that day, like her hair, her nails, and her makeup. Yes, that will take up her entire day. But you: Besides a few added maneuvers in hygiene such as flossing, cutting your toenails, and splashing on aftershave, you will have nothing to fill your day from the moment you wake up to the time you put on your monkey suit.

So be sure to plan ahead. One organized groom with a 6:00 p.m. Saturday wedding decided to host all his groomsmen in a mini golf tournament. The two foursomes killed 5 full hours between 18 holes of golf and a pre-celebratory toast on the 19th—filling the groom's whole day. Relaxing and therapeutic, the activity kept the groom's mind off the coming events.

Tired of living in a golfers' world? Yes, there are other activities than golf to pass a summer day. (But we challenge you to find one that takes any longer; why do you think so many golfers are married men?) Whatever your sport— bicycling, running, basketball, tennis—just do it. The physical activity will relieve stress and tension and will give you something besides the wedding to focus on. If you find sports to be the most unrelaxing thing in the world to pursue, or it's the dead of winter, rent all three *Godfather*s with your best man, order some pizzas, and set the alarm.

Nuptial No No

No matter what time you're getting married, get a good night's sleep before the wedding—especially if your rehearsal dinner is the night before. Even though you might be tempted to stay out late with your friends, you will be very unhappy with a bad hangover on your wedding day.

The point is to pursue some activity that won't have you ruminating about the events to come. If your idea of relaxing is having a few beers, heed this warning: A "few" is two or three over a couple of hours on a full stomach. On your wedding day, subtract one from that total. No one will be overly pleased with you if you show up buzzed to your own wedding. Besides, there's plenty of time for drinking right *after* the ceremony....

The following are some stress-relief tips for your wedding day and beyond:

➤ Pursue physical activity. The endorphins released in your body have a positive physical effect on you, making you feel more confident, relaxed, and energized.

➤ If your mind is racing, pursue an activity that will distract you. Hang out with your best man and tell old stories. Play poker with your groomsmen. Rent a funny movie. Watch a sports event.

➤ Help your bride with last-minute finishing touches. If she's made some decorations herself, help put them up. If she and her family are doing any of the cooking, offer your assistance. Just don't see her in her dress ahead of time; it's supposed to be bad luck.

➤ Spend some time with your parents. They will appreciate the sentimentality of the moments just before their little boy becomes a man. Of course, if your parents have a tendency to drive you insane, do not add unnecessary stress to your day.

➤ Avoid excessive caffeine, alcohol, nicotine, and sugar. Too much of any of them, and you'll feel jittery or sleepy or you will crash from a sugar high.

➤ On the other hand, don't decide that this is the day you'll quit smoking.

➤ Read a good book.

➤ Meditate.

➤ Get a massage. If you've never had one, get over your fears. There is nothing more relaxing than a good full-body massage.

➤ Do some hard physical labor, such as moving furniture to your new house or putting up drywall. But don't do anything that might violate your physical integrity; we're thinking back injury, broken toe, sprained anything. Your bride might never forgive you for ruining the video by gimping down the aisle (which may be a sign in itself).

Icy Toes

It is natural for both men and women to experience "cold feet" immediately preceding their wedding. This is when you start violently doubting the wisdom of your idea to marry. Especially for men, it is quite normal; after all, it's going against the absolute fabric of masculinity to marry, violating traits such as independence and "playing the field." With all the pressure immediately preceding your ceremony, you might be inclined to doubt your decision. If this happens, get it off your chest—or just get over it. Your fears are being magnified by the intense pressure of the day. Unless you've come to a sudden epiphany backed up by solid evidence of wrongdoing by your fiancée, your feelings will fade once the pressure's off.

Groom Gambit

A strategy to follow if you get cold feet just before the wedding: Fill your mind with positive images of your bride—the time she took care of you when you were sick, how happy she was the day you proposed, how good she is with your nieces and nephews.

Wedding Day Agenda

At your wedding, it's wise to set up some sort of day's agenda for you, your bride, and your close family members to know in advance. You should figure out timing; will there be a lag between the ceremony and reception for photos? If so, where will guests go in between? It's nice to avoid this lag if you can, but if constraints on your ceremony or reception site are tight, you might have to suck it up. For you and your wedding party, it'll probably mean a photo session—but with some tunes from the limo and a little celebratory champagne, you can start the party a little early. As for your guests, you might want to have a close relative or friend host a pre-wedding soireé where guests are welcome to hang out if they so desire. Or you might want to propose some options for activities—a nearby park where they can take a walk, a museum, or a coffeehouse.

Once you've arrived at the reception after the ceremony, there should be some sequence of events to move the night along. If you're having a fairly typical traditional wedding, that sequence consists of a receiving line, the introduction of the wedding party, a cocktail hour, dinner, and then dancing. Sprinkled within are the cake cutting, a pre- or post-dinner toast from the best man and the bride's father, and the toss of the bouquet. You can include or subtract events, as well, depending on how you're structuring your party. Remember, it's your wedding. If you don't want to incorporate certain traditions, you don't have to.

Wedding Traditions

Some traditions are so ingrained in the institution of marriage that it would be difficult to break from them—such as the engagement ring or the wedding cake. But couples seem to be sloughing off other traditions, depending on their personal preferences, such as the receiving line and the bouquet toss. Your ethnic background, geographic region, and personal style will contribute greatly to these decisions. In the meantime, the following wedding traditions and their origins might help you decide.

The Engagement and Wedding Rings

There are geographic and time variations on the genesis of the engagement ring. The earliest evidence of a wedding ring comes from archeological finds in ancient Egypt. Bands of gold were by far the most valuable, and as circles, they symbolized eternity—having no beginning and no end.

Early evidence of the engagement ring for Roman Catholics appeared in 860 A.D., when Pope Nicholas I decreed that an engagement ring become a required statement of nuptial intent. As a devotee to the sanctity of marriage, the Pope required that the ring be of some valued metal, preferably gold, which would represent a financial sacrifice for the groom. That era was also marked by serious punishments if a promise of marriage was broken, including excommunication of men or banishment of women to a nunnery.

Evidence of history's early diamond engagement rings comes from 15th century Venice, where it was discovered that the diamond is one of the hardest, most enduring substances in nature. Toward the end of the 15th century, diamond rings of gold and silver became popular promises of engagement among wealthy Venetians.

The Wedding Cake

Wedding cakes were not always the opulent, frosted concoctions you see today. In fact, wedding cakes were not even originally for eating; they were for throwing at the bride. In the first century B.C., throwing cake at the bride was a symbol of fertility incorporated into traditional wedding ceremonies. Perhaps that's one explanation for the obnoxious "tradition" of the wedding couple smooshing cake in each others' faces following the cake cutting.

Evidence of the modern wedding cake comes from 17th century Britain. The tradition at the time was to pile baked goods, including scones and biscuits contributed by guests, in a heap; the larger the heap, the more fortunate the new marriage. It's rumored that a visiting French chef was appalled by this abundance of bland baked goods and pursued the opposite route—creating an iced, multi-tiered cake sensation. At first, the British balked at such overt excess, but the tradition quickly caught on and has remained to this day.

The Honeymoon

It's doubtful that this is one of the traditions you'll want to break. But in fact, at one time honeymoons were anything but the blissful, romantic getaways they are today. The word comes from the early Christian era in Scandinavia, when men abducted women as brides from neighboring villages. The man and his bride would go into hiding for a period of time, during which their location was known only to the best man. They would remain in hiding until the bride's family ended its search; the couple would then return to his own people.

My, but how things have changed. Today, it's questionable whether the man even has to be involved in the honeymoon planning (although if you are following tradition, it is ultimately your responsibility). The nice thing about modern times, however, is that your bride goes on your honeymoon willingly. With any luck, that willingness will last the whole trip.

The Bouquet Toss

At its inception, the bouquet was a symbol of happiness. Today, it's thrown over the bride's shoulder to an audience of the unmarried women attending the wedding. Whoever catches the bouquet is said to be the next to marry. Some women choose not to participate because it is a glaring reminder of who among the women are single and who are attached. And some women take offense at the implication that they are incomplete without a man. Harmless fun or anti-feminist? You decide.

Throwing the Garter

At some weddings, throwing the garter goes hand-in-hand with tossing the bouquet. The garter is removed from the bride's leg by the groom (often to the sounds of "The Strip") and is then tossed over the groom's shoulder to a collection of unmarried men. The man who catches it then has to slide it up the leg of the woman who caught the bouquet, in front of a rowdy crowd of gawkers who will encourage him to go higher, higher, as the photographer snaps pictures of the whole event. The origin and meaning of this practice is unknown but in time may be credited to late 1900s cheese.

The Chicken Dance

If you are hiring a disc jockey to play your music, you will probably be faced with the question: to chicken dance or not to chicken dance? (For those of you chicken dance virgins, this is a special dance that's goofier than the hokey pokey and sillier than the Electric Slide, though similar in its group orientation.) Those of our parents' generation seem to enjoy its wacky essence; in my cousin's wedding, this issue was a major point of contention between the bride and her father. Once again, it is ultimately up to you.

Clink-of-Glass Smooching

Traditionally, clinking guests' glasses with silverware during the reception dinner is a signal for the groom to kiss his new wife. They clink, you kiss. There have been weddings where this becomes out of hand, and the wedding couple barely has time to eat during an unreasonable number of requests. Don't feel you must kiss just because you hear a clink. The clinker could be your smart-aleck nephew or perverted uncle—each of whom have their own agendas. Don't humor them more than you have to.

Writing Your Own Vows

Another wedding day option you might want to consider is writing your own vows, which can personalize your ceremony and make it a bit more unique. Check with your clergy as soon as you can to determine whether there are constraints or guidelines when writing vows of your own. If there are no constraints, here are a few guidelines to help you do it right:

> ➤ **Be personal.** This is the time to address your unique situation. Talk about the special traits that made you fall in love with her, your views on the meaning of marriage, or your excitement about the future together. Sincerity and a bit of forethought go a long way.

> ➤ **Ask the right questions.** When contemplating the content of your vows, ask yourself about your

unique situation and reflect a bit on what this day and your bride really mean to you.

➤ **Keep them short.** Your vows don't have to be a thesis-worthy diatribe on commitment, love, and marriage. A few well-chosen anecdotes go much further than a full exposé of your opinions.

➤ **Remember the seriousness of the event.** It's okay to be playful, but keep things on a relatively solemn level. This is not the time or place for embarrassing stories, intimate details, or references to the more basic aspects of marriage such as money and child-bearing plans.

➤ **Practice, practice, practice.** Read your vows aloud in advance so you're used to the nuances of your words. Be sure to bring a copy of them to your ceremony, or have the clergy read them for you and your bride to repeat. It's easy to forget even the most memorized of speeches under the stress of the occasion.

➤ **Print your vows in your program.** Sometimes, it's difficult for everyone to hear the vows exchanged during the ceremony, and with printed programs, you can be sure everyone experiences them.

Wedding-Day Etiquette

All along, we've been saying it's your day, and you can do what you want. Now we're here to say it's your day—to a limit. Obviously, this event revolves around you and your bride, and it's one of the more important occasions you'll experience. But you should also keep in mind that by having a wedding with invited guests, you are choosing to honor friends and family who you want to share in the celebration. On your wedding day, everyone wants a piece of the bride and groom.

You should heed a few caveats in order to acknowledge your honored guests. The first, which is optional, is the receiving line. The *receiving line,* which can immediately follow the ceremony in church or reconvene at the reception site, consists of you, your bride, and both sets of parents, as well as bridesmaids and groomsmen if that is your wish. You can also limit attendants to best man and maid of honor only.

If parents are divorced, you may choose to have fathers circulate among the guests instead of stand in line. If your father is hosting the wedding, however, you may want him to head the line anyway—simply separate divorced parents within the line to avoid confusion among guests. If you or your bride feel particularly close to step-parents, you may also ask them to receive.

Wedding Words

The **receiving line** is a convenient way to give a warm welcome to friends and family who've come to share your wedding.

The receiving line is meant to ensure that you greet every guest at your wedding. After the ceremony or before the reception, guests will wait patiently in line to tell your bride how beautiful she looks, how happy they are for you, and how nice the ceremony was. (These are the three standard receiving lines; no pun intended.) Some choose to eschew the receiving line because it takes a long time to greet every guest in this fashion and it takes a pro to make engaging small talk with up to a few hundred people in a row, one after the other. Not to mention you must remember names.

Some couples instead choose to greet each table individually following dinner to ensure they haven't missed anyone. This process can go a little faster, and it happens at a time in the evening when everyone's a bit more relaxed. That can make for more meaningful exchanges.

Although you should make the most of enjoying your wedding, you should make some effort to greet most or all of your guests—not only your immediate family and friends.

Thank-You Notes

Acknowledging your guests also transcends the time after your wedding. Yes—it's the dreaded thank-you notes. If you have trouble even writing one for your Great Aunt Millie's annual birthday gift, this task might cause you some trepidation. It is proper etiquette, however, to write half the thank-you notes yourself for wedding gifts received.

Thank-you notes can be ordered with the rest of your stationery (invitations, place cards, and so on). You might get a better deal this way, in volume. Plus, you'll have them on hand immediately following the wedding. Some couples take thank-you cards to write on their honeymoon flight—especially if there's a long trip involved. This way, you can get it out of the way immediately.

Thank-you notes should be handwritten and acknowledge the specific gift you've received and how you'll use it. For example, if you've received a skillet, talk about how you can't wait to use it to make Saturday brunch for your bride. If it's one of 12 place settings, mention how you're looking forward to entertaining. In other words, phrase the notes in such a way that makes the givers feel good.

You should get thank-you notes out as soon as possible. Especially if the giver has ordered your gift from a registry, he or she has no way of knowing it actually arrived at your doorstep until a thank-you note mentions it.

If the idea of writing 100 thank-you notes makes you break out in hives, negotiate this task out to your bride. Offer her something in return for doing all of them; then, you can just sign them at the end. Although it is proper etiquette for the groom to write half of them, it's a safe bet that most guests won't be surprised to receive a thank-you note written in the bride's handwriting. Then, you get what you want, your bride gets something she wants—and everyone is happy. If you become stuck with the task, however, simply refer to Appendix D, "Writing Thank-You Notes They'll Remember," so you can be sure you're doing it right.

Thank-You Gift

Although it's not mandatory, it is awfully nice to acknowledge both sets of parents with gifts following your wedding. Whether they've contributed their finances or their time (or just their egg and sperm), it's nice to show appreciation for all they've done. Some gift ideas include flowers to arrive when you're already gone on your honeymoon; a gift certificate to their favorite restaurant, where they can finally relax with a dinner on you; spa treatments (you'll know whether your father would actually go for that); hobby-related gifts, such as a tennis racket, golf clubs, or an item to add to a special collection; a gift certificate to an inn or hotel to spend some time away together; tickets to a show or concert they'd enjoy; a framed picture of you and them from the wedding or a special wedding "parent's album"; even a card expressing your thanks. It's easy to get caught up in yourselves in the occasion; show your parents that they raised you right with a token of your appreciation.

Chapter 10

Post-Marital Bliss and Blues: Creating a Home

In This Chapter

➤ Couples Financing 101

➤ Making housework work for you

➤ Moving in together

➤ Keeping sparks alive

The wedding day has passed with much fanfare, and the happy hangover from your honeymoon has just about dissipated. Now comes the rude awakening. You still have to go to work every day? You're still having car trouble? Wait, now *she's* having car trouble, and you have to deal with that, too? You might be a married man now, but you still have the same daily annoyances to handle as your former single self—times two, due to your wife's contributions.

Unless you've been living together for a while, marriage will bring some pretty big adjustments. From getting used

to sleeping in the same bed—every single night—to sharing expenses and creating long-term financial goals together, these changes can be both positive and tough to
manage at first. It's these adjustments that will make your
first year of marriage blissful—and might also have you
singin' the blues.

Financing 101

Probably the first big hurdle you will have as a newly married couple is figuring out a financial plan that will be equitable, will maximize your resources, and will make both
of you feel comfortable and secure. Again, things have
changed since your parents' initial union, when financial
matters were more cut and dried. Mr. Cleaver brought
home the majority of the bacon, and June divvied it up
into household expenses. Occasionally, she bought something Dad deemed too expensive, they argued, and Mom
learned her lesson. Or if they were operating outside of
black and white sitcoms, they had brawls that resulted in
real marital problems—problems you would like to avoid
in your own marriage.

How things have changed. More than likely, you and your
bride are both working and have become accustomed to
certain money-management habits. Possibly, you both
have small nest eggs you've saved over the last few years.
Maybe you're lucky enough to have received an inherit-
ance or trust or great returns on investments. This can
make for some tricky financial maneuvering.

If either of you has serious assets (a house, a business, and
so on) in your name already—or serious debt—it might be
wise to consult an experienced financial planner. You'll be
able to put your money to work right away, and he or she
can help you set up a long-term financial strategy. For
smaller potatoes, such as monthly budgeting and saving,
we present some guidelines here that might make life a
little easier.

Groom Gambit

One of the best things you and your wife can do, if your companies offer it, is contribute the maximum allowable amount to your 401(k) plans. This pre-tax income will grow into a retirement fund that will be helpful in alleviating your fears about the Social Security you probably won't be getting when you retire.

Before your wedding even takes place, it's a wise idea to open a dialog about what each of you expects from a financial standpoint. Studies show the two major conflicts facing marriages concern money and sex; setting up a financial plan and budget is a necessity if the two of you are to weather this particular storm. The second problem, of course, you'll never have to give a second thought.

Financial Strategies for Marriage Beginners

Be open and honest. Money is a touchy subject, and you've been told your whole life it's a private one, too. It might seem somewhat unnatural to suddenly be a financial open book with your new wife, especially if you attach a lot of power, security, or value to the accumulation of money. However, it's in your best interest to begin thinking differently now. The reason you got married in the first place is to establish a partnership that would be mutually advantageous in the various areas—including financially. You should both come clean now about your assets and liabilities if you want to realistically plan for the future.

Goals

Set your goals. Whether it is a house, a sabbatical to Europe, or children for which you want to begin saving, it's a good idea to set these priorities in advance. Once you have mutually established goals, it's much easier to achieve them; otherwise, the point of saving can be somewhat lost. Decide how much you will need to save in order to achieve these goals, and then set up a monthly savings plan in a joint account to which you will both contribute. If your wife isn't working outside the home (and thus won't contribute financially), it's still wise to plan these objectives together so you're working toward a common goal.

Current Expenses

Establish parameters for *fixed* and *variable expenses*. If you make twice as much money as she does, it's not reasonable to expect a 50/50 split on expenses such as rent or mortgage, car payments, or entertainment. Experts recommend that you divide these expenses to reflect the differences in your income levels. For example, if your monthly rent is $1,000, and you make $60,000, but she brings home $30,000, you should pay twice the amount she does; in this case, approximately $650 to her $350. (If you're really anal, the more proper breakdown would be $666.66 and $333.33—but this type of hair-splitting is not recommended for a harmonious marriage. It's kind of reminiscent of that annoying couple who brings a calculator when they join you at a restaurant so they can figure out right down to the penny exactly how much everyone owes.)

Wedding Words

A **fixed expense** is one that remains the same from month to month, such as rent, student loan payments, or your cable bill. A **variable expense** changes from month to month and can include such expenses as meals out, sporting events, clothing, or travel.

Joint Accounts

Set up a joint account for all joint fixed expenses, including rent or mortgage, household expenses such as bills, furniture, and groceries, vacation savings, car payments, and entertainment. Keep individual accounts for personal or variable expenses, such as clothing, sports equipment or fees, and individual entertainment, and establish a budget in advance to determine how much each of you will put toward those costs. This plan will help you avoid conflict in the future. For example, if after joint expenses, bills, and joint savings, you each have $300 a month in funny money, that money is yours to spend or save at your discretion. That way, she won't complain if you buy a new Big Bertha driver, and you won't question her choice in buying a new pair of $150 Joan and David shoes. Plus, if there's some big-ticket item the two of you will just never agree upon (such as a boat or sports season tickets), you can use this account to save for it separately. She can save up for a spa vacation with her best friend. No complaints.

Who Signs the Checks?

Establish parameters if one of you is the sole breadwinner. If you're the one bringing home the dough, do not expect to control every dollar that leaves your household. Again, the key is setting up a budget of fixed expenses and establishing a set amount of money she can use at her discretion—whether it's for clothing, a gym membership, or saving for a rainy day. Especially if she's had earning power in the past and has given it up to be a stay-at-home wife or mom, it's best to set up some kind of independent fund she can use with impunity. If the situation is reversed, and you're the stay-at-home dad, the same rules apply.

You can also choose the traditional route, and have just one checking account from which all funds come and go. Hey, your parents made this work (that is, if they're still married); why can't you? This arrangement probably works better for younger couples with little savings and fewer spending habits to break and for couples with very common financial goals and spending habits. Otherwise, there might be some resentment about who's spending what.

Nuptial No-No

Avoid racking up credit card debt early in your marriage (or ever, for that matter). Don't make wedding or household purchases that you wouldn't be able to afford without credit. You'll end up paying for that big-screen TV three times by the time you've paid off all the interest.

Money Troubles—Not Us!

You will inevitably conflict about money at some point in your relationship. If you don't, you might want to recheck whether yours is a Stepford wife. Behavior about money is more deeply and psychologically ingrained than you might ever think, and attitudes are established with your early experiences concerning money. Ever wonder why your grandparents are so conservative, saving a lot and wasting little? Chances are they lived through the Depression, when money, food, and other necessities were so scarce that people were forced to develop these habits. To them, credit card debt is unnecessary and foreign. It's a sharp contrast to our generation, raised to take for granted our many luxuries that our grandparents worked their whole lives for.

The point is that you might have very different attitudes about saving, spending, and managing money. To you, food that spoils in the refrigerator is a travesty; to her, eating three bites of her $27 entré is the norm. Do not let little things such as this get under your skin; you were brought up differently, and it's up to you as a couple to make these differences work for you, not against you.

It's Never Too Early to Start Investing

Don't forget about investing. It's eminently more profitable than socking your money away in a bank or bonds. Although it may be intimidating at first, if you approach the stock market as a long-term investor, you have little to worry about. History shows that your money will almost inevitably grow, unless you choose an ultra-risky investment. If you want to play the stock market like a roulette wheel, however, you've got a new set of problems. If you do decide to invest in the market, you'll need to secure a broker or learn a bit about your online options, such as eTrade, which can be extremely cost effective.

Talk It Over

Ultimately, communication and respect are priorities when it comes to managing money with a partner. Unless your wife is a complete control freak, or irresponsible and childlike, you should be able to have a reasonable exchange concerning expenses and money.

Making Housework Work for You

Revelation number two about living together: You have different habits when it comes to cleaning and organizing your household. You quickly realize that you cannot comprehend her stress over your leaving one dirty dish in the sink, and she is dumbfounded by the fact that a toilet brush is as foreign to you as E.T. To survive this storm, you will need to learn how to play her Felix to your Oscar. Why do you think so many couples who live together never get married?

The simple truth is that no one really likes housework. People just have different tolerances for how much dirt and disorder they can live with. Housework might be a source of pride, a vehicle for relieving stress, a compelling force—but no one actually *likes* it, no matter what they claim.

There are some tasks that you might dislike more than others. Scrubbing the bathtub might be infinitely more distasteful, than, say, taking responsibility for the garbage. Your job as a newly married couple is to divvy up these chores according to what each of you prefers to do. She does the laundry and dishes; you vacuum and dust. She mows the lawn; you maintain the cars. Set up a fairly equitable balance of tasks that each of you will take responsibility for.

Groom Gambit

Women's three greatest housework pet peeves: Don't leave a dish in the sink if you can wash it or put it in the dish-washer. Clean off your whisker shavings from the sink bowl. And always put the toilet seat down. (There's nothing worse than sitting on cold porcelain in the darkness of 3 a.m.)

Once you've done that, you should set up a schedule. If she's responsible for the kitchen and you the bathroom, establish a weekly or biweekly cleaning schedule and stick to it. If it's easier, post it on the refrigerator and check off the dates you're scheduled to clean. If you adhere to your schedule, there are fewer chances of pointless marital conflict.

If you both work outside the home, it's only fair to split household responsibilities evenly. But if one of you is a stay-at-home spouse, it makes sense that she or he should be the individual to take charge of managing the house—and the housework.

If none of the preceding strategies works, or the two of you are just too busy to keep your home as organized as you'd like, it's time to outsource. Bite the bullet and hire a cleaning person, even if it's only for a once-a-month scrub. The few dollars it costs might end up saving you a lot of heartache. Split the cost and stop arguing. If it's laundry that's got you down, most Laundromats now have drop-off service—a.k.a. bachelor bundles—where you can pay someone else to do your laundry. Just drop it off in the morning and it's ready after work, fabric-softener fresh and crisply folded. This is especially great for apartment dwellers with no laundry facilities on site. But beware: You'll never want to do your own laundry again.

Moving in Together

Before you can have any of the preceding conflicts, it's necessary to establish a living space. If one of you already has a rent-controlled apartment with no rental-fee increase since 1969, your choice is pretty obvious. But if you're both living with roommates (or at home), it will be necessary to find new digs. This is the fun part of getting married—unless, of course, you're in financial straits and you end up living with the in-laws. In that case, you're in no position to get married anyway.

Groom Gambit

Do your homework before you buy a house. Research tax levels in different municipalities, consult with financial institutions for breaks for first-time buyers, and choose a realtor who you trust will give you some honest answers and good advice. Ask recent home buyers about strategies and breaks they've encountered, and consult your parents on this one. They know a lot about mortgages.

First, you will be amazed at what you can afford together. Unlike finding an apartment with a roommate, all you'll need is a one-bedroom apartment—which can make your rent dollars go a lot further, especially if you're looking in a high-rent city such as New York or San Francisco. If it's a house you've wanted but have been holding back pending more stability and permanence in your life, you can now go hog-wild. You might want to start searching for your dream pad before your wedding so you can have your home relatively established (or at least freshly painted) before you get back from your honeymoon.

If you're already living together, you also might want to consider moving. If you've been cohabiting for a while, you probably already realize that not whole lot will change once you're married; presumably, you've already been sharing finances, housework, and sleeping arrangements. It's a good idea to have some change in pace to mark this new stage in life (and to house all the booty you receive as wedding gifts). Picture coming home from the excitement of your wedding and honeymoon to the same old messy apartment, same job, same life. Kind of depressing, isn't it? It might make a move to a new place worthwhile.

Keeping Sparks Alive

One of the greatest ironies about the institution of marriage is that the time leading up to engagement and marriage are full of happiness, anticipation, and excitement, but then shortly thereafter, many couples complain incessantly about the trappings of marriage. Either these complainers have married the wrong person, or they fall under the umbrella of "no boring situations, only boring people." In other words, everything in life is what you make of it. If you wined and dined your wife while you were courting but now find comfort and contentment in take-out every Friday night, of course she'll feel resentful. If she suddenly stops shaving her legs, you might not be pleased. The secret to many strong marriages is that the participants don't take each other for granted. The following are a few strategies to help keep that initial romance alive:

➤ Continue to go on dates. Once you're living together, the dynamics of social life and entertainment change. Sometimes, it's just easier to stay home, order a pizza, and hope for a good HBO movie. But there's something to be said for setting up "dates" a few days in advance. Call your wife at work early in the week and set up a weekend date. Then, pick a new restaurant, club, or nearby tourist spot that neither of you has seen and test the waters. It might sound a little corny, but you'll create a bit more excitement and *romance* than another last-minute trip to the local multiplex does.

Wedding Words

Romance, as defined by the *Oxford Desk Dictionary,* is "fantasy, mystery, nostalgia, glamour, exoticism." As defined by the majority of married women, it's the thing that ends on their wedding day. To keep her on her toes, do something unexpected every once in a while, such as bring home flowers or surprise her with a little gift.

➤ Close the bathroom door. In other words, maintain some semblance of privacy and civility. Although one of the beauties of marriage is having that one person you feel infinitely comfortable with, it's best not to push the issue. Don't resort to behaviors you kept under control while you were dating—belching, swearing, showing bad table manners, and so on. There's no quicker way to take the magic and mystery out of a relationship.

➤ If you feel a rut coming on, fill it. It's easy for hum-drum routines to take over your daily life, with weeks and months that'll make you feel like Bill Murray in *Groundhog Day.* When this malaise begins taking over, take the reins and infuse some fun into your routine. If you went away a few weekends a year while you were dating, continue to do so. If you used to have a regular tennis date, keep it up. The object is to continue to do the things you enjoyed together from the start, without letting life's responsibilities overwhelm you.

In Conclusion

You've been presented with a lot of facts, figures, and advice in these pages—not to mention the unsolicited advice you've received from your fiancée, mother, clergyman, and caterer. Overwhelmed? Don't let yourself be. The key to all this wedding madness is to remain patient, be prepared, and do your best. It'll help you sleep well at night and get your marriage off to a healthy start. When things get too crazy, consider yourself lucky; you'll never have to scramble for a Saturday-night date again.

Chapter 11

Real Grooms, Real Stories

In This Chapter

➤ Imbibing on your wedding day

➤ Irresponsible wedding day behavior

➤ The groom who did it all

➤ Speaking up on your bride's behalf

➤ The groom who did it without his parents' blessing

➤ Ready for monogamy

Suddenly, you feel so alone. Before you were engaged, it seemed as if all your friends were getting married; now it seems as if they're all swinging singles. You have concerns, hopes, and fears, but you can't talk to any of your guy friends about it—and your bride-to-be would freak out if she knew some of the things on your mind. You're afraid this unusual pre-marriage state of mind will begin affecting your behavior and that it will come out on your wedding day. We're here to tell you you're not alone.

Plenty of grooms have experienced wedding day jitters and mishaps. Here are their stories.

The Groom Who Drank Too Much

A groom from Memphis, Tennessee, was engaged to be married to the girl of his dreams. He was a country music producer, she was a kindergarten teacher. They had met at the large Southern state college they both attended, where he worshipped her for three years before she even knew he existed. When he finally got up the courage to introduce himself, they became virtually inseparable. At college he was a football player and she was president of her sorority. Both high achievers and plugged in socially, this couple worked hard and played hard. Since their college days, however, neither of them partied much anymore. They had careers to keep them busy and each other to keep them happy.

Along came their wedding day and the groom was nervous. Not because he thought he was making a mistake, but because he hated being "on stage." Their wedding guest list numbered a hefty 400 people, most of whom he did not know. The thought of making small talk in a receiving line with so many people put him into a cold sweat. The thought of standing and speaking at the altar in front of them actually made him light-headed. He consulted his best man for advice as he dressed for the wedding.

His best man, a football player buddy from college, had just the solution. He pulled out a flask and encouraged the groom to take a sip to calm his nerves. Unfortunately, the groom went too far and finished off the flask, only to remember he hadn't eaten anything that day. But hey, he felt great! Of course, he doesn't think he'll watch his wedding video again any time soon—seeing himself stumble on his way up to the altar was a one-time viewing only.

And he wishes he remembered more of the ceremony and reception. So does his bride.

Nuptial No-Nos

Take it easy on the spirits before and during your wedding festivities—you don't want the "happiest day of your life" to be the one you don't remember. If you're nervous before the wedding, try some natural relaxation techniques—deep breathing, meditating, exercise, or a distracting activity. Lay off the liquor until you're already married.

The Groom Who Drank Too Little

Alison fell in love with her groom in New York City because he was very sensible and serious, not like the "boys" she encountered at the bars her friends liked to go to. He had put himself through college and law school on his own, secured a position at one of the better firms in the city, and devoted himself to a career. He was the type of guy who does what he says he's going to do—friends can always rely on him and he calls his mother regularly. So when it came to his wedding, he helped his bride plan much of it so that the burden didn't fall solely on her, and worried over the details almost as much as she did. "Were all the responses received? Has the band gotten the playlist yet? Are our honeymoon reservations confirmed?" Okay, some might call him anal. His bride called him Andy.

On his wedding day, Andy was well prepared. His tuxedo fit like a tapered glove, his week-old hair cut had grown out just enough, and he managed to shave with no nicks.

He arrived at the church not on time, but early. He watched from the vestibule as the guests arrived, worrying that he wouldn't get to talk to all of them. When he greeted his bride as she met him at the end of the aisle, the ceremony went off without a hitch.

And so did the reception. But the bride soon realized that "no hitches" and "fun" were not necessarily synonymous. In fact, she barely spent time with her groom all evening. Andy was busy making sure he greeted and conversed meaningful with each and every person. Now, there's nothing wrong with being polite, she thought, but polite to a fault was a problem. She only danced two songs with him, and she knew he didn't relax and enjoy the fruits of their laborious planning all evening. The bottom line? She knew he'd be a good provider, but he might need loosening up a bit on the social side.

Groom Gambit

Don't forget to enjoy your wedding! Don't get caught up in the "obligation" portion of the wedding, forgetting to whisk off the bride every so often for a dance or a stolen kiss. Don't let the evening end before it's even really begun.

The Groom Who Didn't Show Up

Tom and Laurie were in love. Or so Laurie thought. They had met through mutual friends and dated for two years before Tom asked her to marry him, after a little encouragement (if that's what they're calling ultimatums these days) from Laurie. During the year-long engagement Tom found himself voluntarily on the planning sidelines, while Laurie and her mother planned the royal wedding:

hundreds of guests, white tie, multiple ice sculptures, flowers flown in from the French countryside. In other words, the wedding Laurie had always dreamed of flaunting in her friends' faces.

Tom had little to say but did as he was told. He bought his tuxedo. He planned a three-week honeymoon to the South Pacific islands. And a subconscious nagging slowly evolved into outright wonderment as to why he had ever thought Laurie was his soulmate. She bossed him around. His friends couldn't stand her. And she cared less about him, he knew, than his year-end bonus.

But Tom thought it was too late to back out. After all, the wedding was planned. The announcement had appeared in the newspaper. Guests had bought their plane tickets. There was nothing he could do now except make the best of an unfortunate situation.

But when he woke up on his wedding day soaked with sweat and remembered his dream of Laurie turning into a wolf and trying to eat him alive, he knew he couldn't go through with it. So he didn't. He simply took the plane ticket, called his best man, and treated him to a trip to Bora Bora.

Nuptial No No

If you're not sure you've made the right decision, confide in a close friend. You're probably just having cold feet, which happens to the best of grooms on their wedding days. But by all means, don't stiff your bride at the altar.

Now, gentlemen—we don't recommend trying this at home, as it is extremely dangerous. While he was away most of his earthly goods were destroyed, though he was never able to prove to authorities that it was Laurie. Plus, 500 wedding guests think he's a total loser. The bottom line? If you're going to cancel your wedding, give some advance warning. Whether you're justified or not, canceling at the last minute is simply bad form.

The Groom Who Did It All

Between Josh and Suzanne, Josh was the organized one. To Josh, clutter and disorganization were the enemy, so he generally established the plans in their relationship. For example, when proposed, he created a "scavenger hunt" for Suzanne, with a series of clues she had to follow all over their small town in order to find him waiting with the engagement ring. His game was so extravagant it took her 2^1/$_2$ hours to finish it, whereby he drove her into the city to have dinner and a romantic getaway at one of the nicest hotels in town. Now, this kind of proposal takes patience and hard work, which Josh had in abundance.

Wedding Words

A **control freak** is a person who cannot allow any decision to be made without his or her say-so. Even if your bride is doing much of the planning but you feel compelled to give the final stamp of approval on every little detail, you qualify. Trust your bride. She may actually have a worthy opinion.

When it came time to plan the wedding, Josh was eager and willing to take on the task. Though his friends couldn't figure out why he'd ever get involved in more than he was forced to, Josh felt compelled to find the best vendors at the lowest prices, which took some serious leg-work. At first, Suzanne was pleased with the arrangement, but then she began to resent her exclusion from her own wedding plans. After all, wasn't she the one supposed to be making these decisions? It came to the point that even when Josh chose a band she loved to play at the wedding, she felt resentful because it was *his* decision. She began wondering whether Josh was a *control freak* who would need to take over everything for the rest of their lives.

The Groom Who Married Without His Parents' Blessing

David and Kristen were like two peas in a pod. They both loved to ski, they wouldn't miss a Chicago Bears game, and neither of them could get enough Thai food. They were meant for each other.

Except for one little factor. David was Jewish, and Kristen was Catholic. Neither set of parents approved of the fact that they were dating, even though they thought highly of the individuals. When they became engaged, however, all hell broke lose.

David's parents tried to stop the wedding any way they could. They threatened to lock him up or disown him (melodrama was a family trait). When it came down to it, though, David wouldn't budge. He loved Kristen, and he knew they would work hard to raise their children to learn both faiths, but more importantly, to be good people. So they eloped, and broke the news to both sets of parents when they returned home.

Faced with the inevitable, David's parents eventually lightened up. They now accept Kristen in their lives, and actually threw a post-wedding reception for the couple a few months later, introducing the couple to friends and family—the ultimate acceptance.

Groom Gambit

Tread carefully when it comes to inter-faith romances.
What your parents seem cool about today might change
drastically once you're engaged. Diplomacy is the key to
harmony, and don't give up on your parents.

The Groom Who Never Spoke Up

Chloe was a strong woman. That's what Burt found so attractive about her. Chloe was a woman who knew what
she wanted and when she wanted it, though she wasn't
brash or rude about it. In fact, she was one of the most
diplomatic people Burt had ever met.

Burt recognized that maybe this attraction was somewhat Freudian in nature. His mother, too, was quite
headstrong—she'd had to be, as a corporate lawyer in
New York City. She was also quite involved in her
children's lives—she was a disciplinarian, a confidante,
and a trouble-shooter all wrapped into one. It was no
wonder that when Burt announced he was getting
married, it was all she could do to resist taking a leave
of absence to help plan the wedding.

Chloe, of course, had her own ideas. She had envisioned
almost every aspect of her wedding for many years, and
already knew the place, the flowers, the music, and the
cake she wanted. Not to mention her mother had some
ideas, too. So when her future mother-in-law began making request after request to change various aspects of the
wedding, in a decidedly unsubtle way, Chloe began getting frustrated.

It came to a head when her mother, who was trying to plan a shower, presented Burt's mother with a list of three different days they could have it, based on a number of considerations including the bridesmaids' schedules, as well as her own. When Burt's mother insisted that none of these dates would do because they interfered with her tennis schedule, Chloe decided she had had enough. She called on Burt to put his mother in her place. After all, it was their wedding, and Chloe's parents were paying for it.

But Burt wouldn't say boo. He refused to get in the middle, which only incited Chloe more. Finally the normally diplomatic Chloe hashed it out with her future mother-in-law in a phone call that both of them would like to forget. After that, mom-in-law kept a much lower profile, but the tension remained well past the wedding day.

Groom Gambit

Don't wuss out on your bride, especially during this stressful time. Any mother-in-law knows that the less she has to say about her son's wedding plans, the better. If she insists on being overly opinionated, it's up to you to diplomatically intervene to prevent unnecessary long-term conflict between your bride and your mother.

The Groom Who Wasn't Ready for Monogamy

For his whole life, Phillip had never wanted for anything—his grandfather's oil investments had made life very comfortable for the family. He had grown up on a 25,000 acre horse ranch outside of Dallas, been schooled in the best New England boarding schools, spent his summers in Europe, and was accepted into Yale despite his less-than-stellar grades, as his dad was an alumnus.

When Phillip met Cassandra at Yale, he thought she resembled a modern-day Grace Kelly—and so did everyone else. She was from a "good" family herself; he laid on the full-court press until she succumbed. They became the golden couple at Yale, and everyone wondered how far from perfect their children could actually end up.

The years went on, Phillip finished business school, and finally proposed to Cassandra. She delightedly accepted, quickly beginning her plans by asking 11 of her closest friends to act as bridesmaids. At the time, she did not know that one would betray her.

Phillip, in the meantime, had gotten bored with Cassandra. He began drinking and carousing until all hours at Manhattan bars and clubs while Cassandra planned the wedding. When he ran into Lily one night, her maid-of-honor, he realized he had never noticed how attractive she really was. We'll spare you the rest of the lurid details.

Nuptial No-No

As any man with a brain knows, stay away from the maid-of-honor. (It's much too close to home.) Of course, the real moral is that if you're not ready to be monogamous, then simply don't get married. You'll save everyone a lot of grief in the long run.

As we're all aware, in a group of friends it's tough to keep a secret. Cassandra found out the bad news at the wedding reception, when a concerned friend thought she ought to know before it was too late (why she hadn't told her 3 hours before is anyone's guess). Regardless, after a few glasses of wine, Cassandra decided it was time everyone knew, and she broke the news in front of much of Manhattan/Dallas society. Needless to say, Cassandra's dad has made it difficult for Phillip to eat lunch in that town again.

The Groom Who Did His Best

Inevitably, you will run into some type of problem during the planning and execution of your wedding. These grooms' stories are only meant to illustrate that the better the planning, diplomacy, and behavior, the more successful your wedding and ensuing marriage will be. The key is making the stuff within your control go smoothly, because there's enough already out of your control to send you for a tailspin. And our most important advice yet? Hang on to your sense of humor. If ever you needed it, it's now.

Glossary

All-inclusive resort   A resort that offers a pay-one-price package deal that includes such amenities as airfare, accommodations, meals, drinks, and sports and activities. Be sure to verify the details. The beauty of all-inclusives is that there are no hidden costs; you don't have to think about money once you're there, even for tipping. Popular resorts include Sandals, Super Clubs, Breezes, Couples, and Club Med.

Attendants   The friends or family members you have chosen to stand up with you at the wedding ceremony. The *groomsmen* act as *ushers,* seating people at the wedding and rolling out the runner for the bride. The best man is a special groomsman.

Best man   The best man is your most honored friend or relative. He will act as your primary support during the wedding and may plan the bachelor party and give a wedding-day toast.

Constructive communication   Constructive communication is meant not to "win" a discussion or put someone on the defensive; rather, it's a style that aims to positively exchange ideas and solve problems.

Dowry   A dowry was traditionally a gift of goods or money given from the bride's family to the groom to make marriage more attractive. The practice is all but obsolete (unfortunately for you...).

Fixed expense   An expense that remains the same from month to month, such as rent, student loan payments, or your cable bill.

Food stations   Term used to describe receptions that are typically cocktail party-style—less structured, with a bar that generally stays open all evening and no defined place settings.

Groom   A groom is an engaged man on the days up to and slightly after his wedding ceremon3y. The *Webster's II New Riverside Pocket Dictionary* has some other definitions for *groom*, too—"to make neat and trim, brush," and "to train."

Groomsman   See *Attendants*.

Registering   The process of creating a "wish list" of household items you'd like to receive as wedding and shower gifts, through a department or specialty store or both. Registering makes guests' choices of gifts easy and guarantees that you'll receive the items you need in the right quantities.

Romance   As defined by the *Oxford Desk Dictionary*, romance is "fantasy, mystery, nostalgia, glamour, exoticism." As defined by the majority of married women, it's the thing that ends on their wedding day. To keep her on her toes, do something unexpected every once in a while such as bring home flowers or surprise her with a little gift.

Usher   See *Attendants*.

Variable expense   An expense that changes from month to month and may include expenses such as meals out, sporting events, clothing, or travel.

Wedding finances   Any wedding-related expenses. Decide before the wedding who will pay for what.

Wedding program   A written document that contains information about the ceremony readings and music, as well as fun information such as wedding attendant profiles. You can customize the program to be as creative as you like.

Appendix B

Wedding Resources

With the incredible number of wedding-related sites online, it's almost impossible to consider what people did for work before life on the World Wide Web. There is an endless number of general wedding sites online, boasting information ranging from etiquette to registry services to ideas for flowers, photography, video, favors, and so on. They all have one thing in common—heavy support from advertisers and online merchants who sponsor and link to these sites hoping for e-commerce. Clearly, these merchants' wishes are coming true because there is no dearth of advertisers or retailers hawking their wares.

Finding wedding sites is as easy as going to any search engine, typing in "weddings," and waiting for the results. But to make your life easier, here are a number of quick tips to get you on your way.

General Sites

www.wednet.com

Comprehensive, nicely organized site with articles, features, and a Q&A forum to answer frequently asked questions.

www.weddingpages.com

Another well-designed and organized site with articles, frequently asked questions, links to other wedding-related sites, downloadable audio featuring wedding songs, and city directories with local vendors. (It does not feature all cities, however; the list items are concentrated in certain regions.)

www.theknot.com

America Online wedding site. Nicely designed, as you would expect from AOL, with wedding "tools" for budgeting, designing invitations, and so on. There's even a relatively comprehensive section for grooms (but of course, you won't need that after finishing this book…).

www.marthastewart.com

Okay, so you say you wouldn't be caught dead on Martha Stewart's site. But as in her magazine, beautiful photography and tasteful ideas for weddings rule this site. If the aesthetic side of you is crying out, this site's for you. Our little secret.

Registry Sites

www.weddingnetwork.com

Offering selections from 30 stores and 45,000 products from china to sporting goods, this registry is about as comprehensive as you'll find anywhere. If you're inviting guests from across the country, online registering can make gift-giving more convenient for everyone.

www.bloomingdales.com

The quintessentially stylish department store also offers an online registry.

www.targetstores.com

Aggressively marketing its wedding registry service, information on Target's Club Wedd service is available online—but you have to visit the store to actually register. Once you get there, all you need to do is sign in, get a bar scanner, and go nuts; all your gift choices are automatically entered into the computerized system once you "zap" them with the scanner. If you've never been to a Target store, you might be surprised by the quality, brand-name stuff they have at more competitive prices; give it a try. The Web site also gives you a full list of

registry possibilities you can print out and use as a check-list to organize yourself ahead of time.

If you like to surf the Net, fewer industries will give you more options than the travel biz. Honeymoon planning is just a subset of the industry. The Internet is a great place to start for ideas on where to go and a quick lesson on how much it will cost you. You can book your vacation right online, but be extremely careful that you're dealing with a reputable company. FYI—the following sites are not supported or endorsed by this book; they've been found the same way you'd find them, and we're just re-porting on our legwork. So tread carefully in all your online dealings.

What's great about the Web is that the information is there to find if you want to use it for price comparisons when dealing with travel agents. Keep in mind that travel agents will do a little more of the homework for you and presumably have a level of expertise and knowledge that will add value to your overall vacation. If all else fails, don't forget your local bookstore, which carries hundreds of travel books that you can buy and take with you. Fodor's guides are particularly good for the inside scoop.

Honeymoon Sites

www.4Honeymoons.com

This is a terrific starting point when planning a honey-moon. When you get to this home page, you'll be greeted with a host of options, including popular destinations, honeymoon registry services, information and resources, and online travel agents. Plus, you'll also find a list of re-lated sites such as 4AirInfo, 4Cruise, and 4Europe.

www.usabride.com

You'll find a lot of sites like this one, which features packages from such major honeymoon resorts as Sandals, Super Clubs, Couples, Breezes, Hedonism II, and Beaches. It's a good site for price comparison.

www.honeymoonsinc.com

This site features mostly Sandals packages but guarantees to have the lowest prices available for your Caribbean honeymoon or wedding.

www.unforgettablehoneymoon.com

Another site dedicated mostly to honeymoon packages, this site seems to offer some more moderately priced packages. If Maui's your destination, the site has a "Maui design-a-package" feature, where you pick your accommodations, activities, and rental car from a list of options; the site will calculate an individual quote for you based on these choices.

www.weddingcircle.com/honeymn/honeymn

A compilation of a large number of Web sites that will help you plan your honeymoon. This site starts out with a menu of choices that includes every continent on the globe; once you choose your continent, the site narrows your choices. This site is another very worthwhile starting point.

Gifts Online

Although it's difficult to swing the proverbial dead cat around on the Web and not be barraged with vendors trying to sell wedding wares, here's a list of gift sites to get you on your way.

www.thegift.com

This site features a lot of gifts for which you can register; it also offers groomsmen's gifts that range from *The Ultimate Guide to Stock Car Tracks* for the gearhead in your life to beer mug sets and computerized putting cups.

http://ultimatewedding.stores

Traditional, economical groomsmen's gifts such as cigar sets, stainless steel flasks, and Swiss Army knives.

www.netique.com

This great site categorizes gifts by special occasions and holidays. It includes groomsmen and wedding gifts, but you might also want to try it for business gifts, Father's Day gifts, or housewarming gifts. A little more upscale in price.

Gift-Giving Guide

It's probably pretty obvious to you by now that exchanging gifts is a large part of the wedding process (and to some, unfortunately, the whole point). Not only will you receive gifts—and probably a lot of them—but you will also be responsible for choosing some—for your bride, your best man, your groomsmen, and your parents. These gifts should be chosen with some care; you should pick items with sentimental or lasting value. In other words, a bottle each of Wild Turkey for your groomsmen ain't gonna cut it.

To help you along with gift ideas for all the important people in your life, here's a quick referral guide in a range of budgets and styles to suit any groom. If the money's just not there after all the wedding expenses, a card with some special words that arrives the morning of your wedding will do nicely.

For the Bride

➤ Jewelry, especially jewelry she can wear on her wedding day. A lovely strand of pearls, pearl or sapphire earrings (something blue), a delicate platinum bracelet—anything goes. She will probably plan ahead what jewelry she's wearing on her wedding day, so you might want to give her your special gift a little early—or prep her that something might be on its way. You can also get her something to wear after the wedding. You know her preferences best, so choose something that she can keep forever.

➤ Something related to a hobby. If she's an avid reader, find a limited, antique, or signed edition of a book by her favorite author. If she paints, get her the upscale brush set she's always wanted but has been too practical to splurge on. A skier might want a new pair of parabolic skis. Whatever her hobby, get something that has meaning and something that will have lasting value.

➤ Something for the house. Maybe it's an original piece of artwork. An antique vanity table. A pretty window box for flowers. Heck, even a dishwasher. Basically, choose anything that will add beauty and make her life easier.

➤ Giftware, such as a beautiful vase or clock from Tiffany's. Or a splurge item from her favorite specialty store.

➤ Spa treatments.

➤ Tickets to a special vacation destination for your first anniversary.

➤ Something handmade or homemade. If you're a writer or artist, create something original to honor the day. If you're great with your hands, build a rocking chair or table. Plant her a garden that will bloom year after year. Extra points count for originality and creativity.

➤ A monthly bouquet of flowers. Online clubs and florists market special plans where you can pre-order and pre-pay for flowers to arrive on your doorstep at regular intervals, such as every month for a year. Drop hints that you'd like the similarly designed beer-of-the-month membership.

➤ Gifts related to specific interests:

Cooking: Gourmet cookware or a set of great cookbooks.

Gardening: Good quality gardening tools. Have them engraved.

Antique collecting: An antique lamp, table, or other piece from her favorite era.

Sports or working out: A home step machine, treadmill, or weight set or inline skates.

Reading: Membership in the literary guild or book-of-the-month club or a book of love poems.

Tennis: New racquet or a club membership for both of you.

Skiing: A cute ski bunny outfit you'd love to see her wear or new skis.

Travel: Plane tickets for a future trip, or reservations at an out-of-town bed and breakfast.

Golf: New clubs, a new bag, or a club membership.

Writing: Elegant stationery, a silver pen, or a laptop computer.

Movies: Limited edition, signed movie poster, a DVD player, or a home theater.

Collecting: A rare or hard-to-find collectible.

Art or home crafts: Lessons or supplies.

Spectator sports: Hockey, football, or basketball season tickets. (Lucky guy.)

Driving: A remote starter for her car, a car CD player, or, if you've got the bucks, an actual car.

Education: First year tuition or money toward classes.

Pretty things: A music or jewelry box, a ring holder, crystal candle sticks, or a vase (although you might receive a lot of these types of items as wedding gifts).

Work: A weekend getaway, a day spa certificate, or a pre-paid massage from a top salon.

Practicality: A needed item for your home such as a couch, table, bedroom, or dining set.

Nightlife: Dinner at the most expensive or exclusive restaurant in town for your six-month anniversary.

You: Luxurious lingerie.

Gifts for Groomsmen

It is standard to honor your groomsmen with a special gift close to your wedding date, as thanks for standing by you during special time. How much you spend is wholly up to you (you might not have much left in your budget after all the wedding expenses)—but grooms have been known to spend anywhere from $20 to $100 (or more) per gift. As you can see, this expense can quickly add up, especially if you have a large wedding party. Don't go totally on the cheap; you want to get a gift that will stand the test of time. But you also don't have to break the bank to buy a tasteful, worthwhile gift. You don't have to choose identical gifts for each groomsmen; in fact, it's proper to give your best man something a little extra.

➤ A silver Swiss Army knife—unless your guys are prone to violence.

➤ A watch. You'll have to splurge a little to get decent ones.

➤ A glass or silver beer stein or flask. Unless your guys have been in rehab (or should be).

➤ A humidor or cigar cutting set. Or a box of Cubans, if you can get them.

➤ Zippo lighters in gold or silver or a unique design.

➤ A silver or gold pen set.

➤ A business card holder. Job required.

➤ A picture frame.

➤ A barbecue set.

➤ An engraved travel mug.

➤ A money clip.

➤ Cuff links or tuxedo studs.

➤ A mini travel bar.

➤ An old-fashioned shaving set.

➤ A wooden dresser-top box for cuff links and tux studs.

➤ A leather shaving bag with initials.

➤ A wine-stopper set.

➤ Silver or leather key rings.

➤ Golf-related gifts.

➤ Gifts from a specialty store, such as a clock in an original design or a chess set.

➤ A portable CD player with individual CDs according to the groomsmen's tastes.

➤ A fun gadget from a store such as The Sharper Image or Hammacher Schlemmer. Think massager, electronic organizer, or golf net for home chipping.

➤ Sports tickets for a future game, to which you can all go together.

➤ A special or limited edition hardcover book.

➤ Suits. Subsidize their purchase instead of asking groomsmen to wear rented tuxes.

Gifts for Parents

Although it's not mandatory, it is awfully nice to acknowledge both sets of parents with a gift following your wedding. Whether they've contributed their finances or their time (or just their egg and sperm), it's nice to show appreciation for all they've done:

➤ Flowers to arrive while you're on your honeymoon. Nothing says "thank you" like flowers.

➤ A gift certificate to their favorite restaurant, where they can finally relax with a dinner on you.

➤ Spa treatments. (You'll know whether your father would actually go for that.)

➤ A gift certificate to an inn or hotel to spend some time away together.

➤ Tickets to a show or concert they'd enjoy.

➤ A framed picture of the four of you from the wedding.

➤ A special wedding "parent's album."

➤ A simple card expressing your thanks.

Writing Thank-You Notes They'll Remember

If you've ever received a thank-you note, you'll understand the subtle difference between one written out of duty and one that has a little more sentimental value. The former sounds like something your mother dictated to you in grade 5 to thank Aunt Mabel for a birthday present; the latter makes a more personal statement.

There's no time like your wedding to learn the difference. Naturally, when you're writing hundreds of thank-you notes in a single sitting, they tend to fall more in the cookie-cutter range than in the homemade apple pie category. This little guide, however, will give you a few tips on writing a proper and well-mannered thank-you note that allows your personality and sincerity to shine through.

Here is an example of the fifth-grade thank-you letter level:

> Dear Aunt Mable,
>
> Thank you dearly for the ceramic ashtray.
> Your kind gesture means a great deal to us.
>
> Love,
>
> Billy

There are a number of things lacking in this letter. The first is any kind of sincerity or personal touch. Even if Billy hates the gift, he should attempt to make some sort of sincere statement about it, such as "it is unique and unusual, and will be a nice addition to our patio." Aunt Mabel's name is also misspelled, which is inexcusable. (If you're unsure of spellings, consult with your mother or another person in the know.)

The following letter illustrates what you should be aiming for in your thank-you notes:

> Dear Aunt Mabel,
>
> Thank you so much for the beautiful silver candelabra. Jody and I have already found a place for it in our new house, on the mantel above the fireplace. A decorator couldn't have found a more perfect piece for the space!
>
> We were so honored you could travel to town for our wedding, and Jody particularly enjoyed meeting you. Can't wait for you to visit next time you're in town.
>
> Talk to you soon.
>
> Love,
>
> Billy and Jody

The bottom line? When writing a thank-you note, pay close attention to the following points:

➤ Double-check the spelling of the person's name.

➤ Use your own language, as if you were speaking face-to-face.

➤ Match up the gift with the giver (be sure to keep meticulous records of who gave you what gift—you will never remember otherwise).

➤ Mention how you'll use the gift.

➤ Include a personal message about your happiness at seeing the recipient of the letter at the wedding. Or, express your regret that he or she was unable to attend.

➤ The note should included the signatures of both you and your bride.

You may want to choose thank-you notes with your initials or a unique design. You can order note cards when you order the wedding invitations and RSVP cards. You may get a reasonable package deal that way.

Top Ten Things to Remember on Your Wedding Day

10. **Eat.** If you're having a buffet or food stations at the reception, it may be difficult to tear yourself away from guests and/or the dance floor. If you're having food stations, ask your best man in advance to make you a plate.

9. **Greet your guests.** Have a receiving line or greet guests at each table individually. You don't have to have an in-depth conversation with every single guest, but it is polite to try to greet as many guests as possible.

8. **Dance.** Don't get so caught up in conversation that you forget to let off a little steam on the dance floor.

7. **Have fun.** You and your families have put a lot of time, effort, and money into the celebration of this union. Make the most of it and enjoy yourself.

6. **Take note of photo opportunities.** Make sure someone takes photos of all close family and friends, especially grandparents, children, out-of-town friends and family, and your entire immediate family.

5. **Thank your parents.** More than likely, they've gone out of their way to help give you this wedding (not to mention raised you). Be sure to express your appreciation.

4. **Spend time with out-of-town guests.** You'll have friends and family at your wedding you see all the time, so make sure to spend enough time with friends and family you don't see as often.

3. **Don't drink and drive.** Arrange for alternate transportation to wherever you are going after the reception well before your wedding day. If the reception is at a hotel, arrange to stay there overnight (many hotels will offer a free room if you hold your wedding reception on the premises).

2. **Have someone keep track of gifts, especially envelopes.** They can easily get misplaced or forgotten in all the excitement. Give this duty to someone you trust, like your best man or a parent.

1. **Kiss the bride.**

Index

90874